VOLCANOES

DATE DUE

Brodart Co.   Cat. # 55 137 001   Printed in USA

D0620006

of related interest

Anger Management Games for Children
Deborah M. Plummer
Illustrated by Jane Serrurier
ISBN 978 1 84310 628 9

How to Be Angry
An Assertive Anger Expression Group Guide for Kids and Teens
Signe Whitson
Foreword by Dr Nicholas J. Long
ISBN 978 1 84905 867 4

The Red Beast
Controlling Anger in Children with Asperger's Syndrome
K.I. Al-Ghani
Illustrated by Haitham Al-Ghani
ISBN 978 1 84310 943 3

Working with Anger and Young People
Nick Luxmoore
ISBN 978 1 84310 466 7

Helping Children to Cope with Change, Stress and Anxiety
A Photocopiable Activities Book
Deborah M. Plummer
Illustrated by Alice Harper
ISBN 978 1 84310 960 0

Games and Activities for Exploring Feelings
Vanessa Rogers
ISBN 978 1 84905 222 1

Cyberbullying
**Activities to Help Children and Teens to Stay Safe in a
Texting, Twittering, Social Networking World**
Vanessa Rogers
ISBN 978 1 84905 105 7

Self-Esteem Games for Children
Deborah M. Plummer
Illustrated by Jane Serrurier
ISBN 978 1 84310 424 7

LITTLE VOLCANOES

Helping Young Children and Their Parents to Deal with Anger

**Warwick Pudney
and Éliane Whitehouse**

Foreword by Tina Rae

Jessica Kingsley *Publishers*
London and Philadelphia

Front cover image source: iStockphoto®.

This edition published in 2012
by Jessica Kingsley Publishers
116 Pentonville Road
London N1 9JB, UK
and
400 Market Street, Suite 400
Philadelphia, PA 19106, USA

www.jkp.com

Originally published in New Zealand in 2003 as *Little Volcanoes* by The Peace Foundation

Copyright © The Peace Foundation 2012
Foreword copyright © Tina Rae 2012

Library of Congress Cataloging in Publication Data
A CIP catalog record for this book is available from the Library of Congress

British Library Cataloguing in Publication Data
A CIP catalogue record for this book is available from the British Library

ISBN 978 1 84905 217 7
eISBN 978 0 85700 595 3

Printed and bound in Great Britain

Dedicated to our children...
Nick, Richard, Jenny, Elizabeth, Alan and their children.

In memory of Éliane Whitehouse.

Acknowledgements

The authors wish to acknowledge the support and assistance of The Peace Foundation of New Zealand, early childhood educators from New Zealand and the parents who are part of our professional experience and as such are part of our learning.

Contents

The Anger Rules

It's OK to feel angry
but think...

Don't hurt others
Don't hurt yourself
Don't hurt property

DO TALK ABOUT IT

Foreword

In 1996, I was given a copy of *A Volcano in my Tummy: Helping Children to Handle Anger* by Elaine Whitehouse and Warwick Pudney. This book became an essential and key resource for me at this time in my work as manager of a behaviour support team in an inner London Local Education Authority. It also inspired me to develop my practice and approaches in terms of working with young people and their carers in an empathic, non-judgemental and solution-focused way alongside developing my own programmes and resources in this area. In this sense, it was a seminal publication for me personally.

An essential element was the underpinning philosophy and motivation of the authors – they wanted to support young people in 'living successfully, healthily, happily, non-violently, with motivation, without fear and with good relationships' (Whitehouse and Pudney 1996, p.5). They sought to encourage individuals to put aside their fear of anger and to begin to 'use' anger in a proactive and productive way.

This hugely informative, practical and comprehensive publication builds still further upon this aim and the authors' guiding philosophy and principles, which I can now place firmly within the framework and context of positive psychology. There is a wealth of insight here regarding the causes of anger and associated behaviours, and the ways in which these can be approached in a truly empathic and effective way. The exercises, tips and strategies (including the use of mindfulness techniques) are entirely practical and evidence based, and are presented with passion, kindness and genuine understanding. This is enormously refreshing in the current social, economic and political climate where parents, carers and those working in the caring professions are often left feeling at fault or inadequate in terms of 'managing' the behaviour and emotional learning of young people.

This publication reinforces the fact that anger is an essential part of being human, and also reinforces Aristotle's challenge to us all 'to be angry with the right person, to the right degree, at the right time, for the right purpose, and in the right way' (Aristotle, *The Nicomachean Ethics*). We know that this is not easy. Essentially, it remains a lifelong challenge for us all, and this truly comprehensive and timely publication will certainly support teachers, parents, carers and young people in recognising, managing and embracing their anger – and the anger of others.

Dr Tina Rae
Educational Psychologist and Academic and Professional Tutor
University of East London
October 2011

Preface

Adults with responsibility for young children often find young children's anger very stressful. This is appropriate as it is an indicator that all is not well in the child's world and that something needs to be attended to. That is the purpose of anger.

Working with that anger, or those who are experiencing it, involves some important concepts and processes.

Below are some of the questions and statements from parents and helping professionals that prompted us to write this book. They are triggers that helpers are often stimulated to respond to.

'I seem to be so angry with my child and I don't know why.'
'We have an angry child in our centre. What do we do?'
'Children seem more angry than they used to be.'
'He's got an anger problem.'

'Anger is bad isn't it?'

'I don't understand why she's angry, this is a happy place.'

'How do I get the parents to see that their fighting affects their child?'

'My child seems angry that I have returned to paid work.'

'I can't stop that child using bad language.'

'We don't have angry children around here.'

'I can't take my child to playgroup because he hits other children.'

'I send an angry child to time out immediately. We are not having any of that here.'

'I'm scared my children will hurt each other.'

'Why do boys have to fight?'

'I keep losing my patience with my children!'

'My two-year-old keeps hurting his baby brother.'

'We need to do something to protect the other children.'

'How do you help the parents see that they need to do something different?'

'My two-year-old throws enormous tantrums.'

In this book we hope that professionals, as well as parents or caregivers, will find information and be able to learn some skills to understand better how to help children process their anger.

Throughout the text the word 'child' is used to describe children of both genders and the use of 'he' and 'she' is alternated. This is done for ease of reference only, and is not intended to reflect any gender bias.

Chapter 1

Beginning at the Beginning

Understanding Child Development and the
Needs of Babies and Small Children

All children are born with a full toolkit of emotions, and each one is valuable for survival. Anger is one emotion, and it is vital to our protection and motivation and as a survival energy source. If our environment takes it away by devaluing it or habitually repressing it, then our happiness and survival are threatened and we may need others to use their anger to save us.

Although anger appears at times of stress and discomfort, and has earned a negative association with hurt, the emotion of anger indicates both unhappiness and the hope of being saved from unhappiness. Consequently, it is a commodity that most of us prefer to use sparingly, best kept for emergencies and to be valued highly.

There is a certain beauty in the natural spontaneous and authentic expression of anger in very young children. It is a major form of communication for young children, and recognizing and understanding it allows us to be better caregivers by noticing their discomfort and responding to it. It is our task to keep it as a form of communication, and to prevent it developing into a choice to behave badly to others; the early years are the best time to intervene in this regard.

Before we are even born, our environment has started to influence us and shape both the use and expression of anger. There is now strong evidence that informs us that the early days, weeks and months of a child's life provide a window of opportunity to establish a child's wellbeing and mental, physical, social and intellectual functioning (Karen 1990a; Perry 1997, 2008, 2009; Schore 1994). For this reason, this chapter does not focus solely on anger, but instead provides an overview of the early development of children and how their experiences can have an impact on later life.

The child's early relationship with the primary caregiver is vital to a sense of wellbeing and safety in the world. The provision of safety, love and the meeting of physical needs reduces stress and anxiety; it reduces not just the need for anger but also establishes a faith in the world as a good place that will influence impulses of fight and flight for the rest of the child's life. Children need to form a secure attachment relationship with their primary caregiver, usually the mother, for at least the first three years.

'Attachment' here means more than holding on to or knowing a person well; it is about an enduring bond that unites an adult and a child in a strong sense of security and belonging through which they both practise trust, empathy and an intuitive togetherness (Bowlby 1973; Fonagy 2001; Karen 1990a; Steele *et al.* 1999).

If this relationship is well formed a child develops an attitude of faith and safety in the world. The brain also develops in such a way that the child is better able to regulate strong emotions such as anger and fear. According to Mark Coen (2011), a clinical social work therapist, secure attachment helps us to:

- feel safe, experiencing comfort and security
- develop meaningful connections with others
- explore our world
- deal with stress
- balance emotions
- repair emotional pain
- make sense of our lives
- create positive memories and expectations of relationships
- challenge ourselves and take healthy risks.

Sometimes things happen that prevent the establishment of a secure parent–child relationship. These might include:

- physical neglect, emotional, physical or sexual abuse
- prolonged or sudden separation from the primary caregiver
- traumatic experiences, such as serious illnesses or accidents
- frequent stress and anxiety
- pre-natal maternal misuse of drugs and/or alcohol
- postnatal addiction to alcohol or drugs where maternal responsiveness is reduced
- changes in foster placements and/or inconsistent or inadequate childcare
- an emotionally unavailable primary caregiver due to isolation or social, hormonal problems
- lack of environmental stimulation for the baby/child
- poor attachment of the mother leaving her unable to attach to the baby.

Helping professionals will have had contact with children who have experienced some of the above. Every effort needs to be made to re-establish the child's sense of safety, and to provide consistency, soothing and connection with the primary caregiver.

We, as part of a community, need to provide support, care and help for parents with small children. Historically, young parents have never had to manage on their own, and should not have to now. If we fail them we will, as a community, suffer the consequences in the years to come.

Symptoms of attachment disorders

Children who suffer from 'attachment disorders' exhibit similar personality traits. The findings of Dr Foster Cline, author of *Understanding and Treating the Severely Disturbed Child* (1979), and Mark Coen (2011), have been combined here, along with our thoughts, to give 25 common warning signs that indicate that a child needs professional help due to a failure to meets those initial needs of love, security and attachment:

- superficially engaging, charming and manipulative
- poor eye contact
- indiscriminately affectionate with strangers
- not cuddly with parents
- destructive to self, others and material things, accident prone
- cruel to animals
- lies about the obvious (wild lying)
- no impulse control (frequently hyperactive)
- learning lags
- lack of cause-and-effect thinking
- lack of conscience, guilt or remorse
- abnormal eating patterns
- poor peer relationships
- preoccupation with fire, blood
- persistent with nonsense questions
- inappropriately demanding and clingy
- abnormal speech patterns
- false abuse allegations
- denial of accountability
- refusal to answer simple questions
- extreme defiance and control issues
- stealing
- mood swings
- sexual acting out
- toileting issues.

Children who are experiencing life changes such as divorce or the death of a family member may experience some or even all of these symptoms. We suggest that if a child exhibits seven or more of these symptoms, professional help should be sought.

Supporting parents

Professionals need to support parents to assist children in developing a secure attachment. Often such behaviours come naturally without guidance. However, parents who did not experience a secure attachment with their own parents will find this more difficult and may need to act more consciously in their parenting (Main, Kaplan and Cassidy 1985; Makinen and Johnson 2006). Parents in this position may find it helpful to see a psychotherapist to help them recognize their behaviour and its effects, and to be able to develop skills of intimacy and trust more consciously.

Some of the parental behaviours that may help a child are:

- responding to a child's emotions by holding, cuddling, crooning, stroking, rocking and mirroring the child's facial and bodily expressions, causing the child to feel safe
- gazing at the child's face and holding eye contact
- responding to the baby's cues of happiness, distress or discomfort
- keeping extended body contact
- over time, verbalizing the child's feelings and associating words with feelings
- demonstrating as a parent that they can sustain the child while the child is distressed, angry or scared until the child is gradually able to sustain herself at such times
- mirroring and enjoying with the child their feelings of joy and excitement so that the child can experience those feelings fully.

In order to have these experiences with a small baby, parents need to feel connected to their child and be in an intimate relationship with the child. This is difficult if:

- a mother is experiencing post-natal depression
- the parents are experiencing difficult relationship problems
- the parents are preoccupied with severe ongoing practical problems
- a parent is violent
- the attaching parent is unable to engage consciously with the child due to a disability, or drug or alcohol misuse.

Professional helpers need to consciously watch and assist when attachment is hindered or even halted. These are the years when training to relate to others takes place, and difficulties in relationships for life may result if nurturing attachment does not take place at this stage.

There are things that professional helpers can do to support parents looking after children during infancy, toddlerhood and early childhood stages, which can help to develop a strong connection with the child.

Pre-birth

There should be a lead maternity carer supporting the mother, such as a midwife, obstetrician or doctor, to nurture the pregnancy's progression.

Signs of affection from both parents, such as talking to the unborn baby and pet names, suggest early bonding. Attitudes of excitement and anticipation are an entitlement for new parents and should not be subsumed in fears for family survival and child wellbeing. Parents may build relationships with the unborn baby by starting a baby book, sharing pictures of the baby's ultrascans, noticing the time of day when the unborn child is most active, noting sounds that the baby responds to, feeling for movement, preparing the baby room, playing music to the developing baby and noticing different responses, talking and singing to the unborn child, holding dreams for who the child will become, and practising on other people's babies. The resolution of any resentment about the pregnancy, from either parent, enables a freedom of connection that is best resolved now to avoid short- or long-term distancing and disconnection.

Attendance at antenatal classes allows another window for the helping professional to notice at-risk parents and refer them for extra support. Classes teach current ways of appropriate nurture. We recommend classes that include fathers in their content and treat them as full partners (Chapman, McIntosh and Mitchell 2000; Diemer 1997; Halle *et al.* 2008; Hanson *et al.* 2009; McElligott 2001; Mitchell and Chapman 2002). Classes can also advise on food and behaviour that may adversely affect a child's development before birth.

Encourage the parents to make the birth of the baby an event for the extended family so that there are better chances of in-built support systems once the baby is born.

Infancy

New mothers are often stunned with the new life that they carry out of a hospital, and speak of feeling overwhelmed as to how to be a good parent. The first six weeks may be times of great fear that they are doing it right, and stress at their inability to stop the baby crying.

Infant homicide rates are high in the first two years (Sedlak and Broadhurst 1996) and helping professionals have the opportunity to act as early detectors of such parental desperation.

Breastfeeding is a great time of literal attachment, and we recommend it for bonding, quite apart from the other reasons commonly used to promote it. Small babies are only able to focus their gaze a short distance – the same distance as that between the mother's eyes and the baby's eyes when the baby is feeding. Most babies will enjoy gazing at their mother and experiencing the play of emotions in their mother's eyes as she gazes back (Ainsworth, Bell and Stayton 1991; Perry 1997; Schore 1994).

Continual holding and body contact builds strong bonds and ensures immediate care and assistance. Some Southeast Asian cultures carry small children until they can walk, thus missing out the crawling stage. A strong sense of continual inclusion in the family results, which challenges the Western need for independence from and for the child. When children are sick, they may be more needy of physical contact, and so if you are working with parents of a sick child in particular, you might consider encouraging continual carrying along with appropriate medical attention. Encourage the parent to hold their baby so that they are facing one another. It is the facial response to a baby and the sound of a familiar voice that helps them to feel secure, understood and connected (Karen 1998).

Soothing distress by rocking and predictive movement helps a child to feel secure, and a rocking chair can also be soothing to stressed parents (Kitzinger 2005). Singing to a baby is also to be encouraged. It is soothing for both the parent and the child. Most cultures have lullabies that have been handed down over generations. Reading simple children's books, particularly those that have repetitive rhythmic passages, can also be a valuable form of bonding.

Infants and toddlers need consistency in their caregivers. This contributes to their sense of security and helps them to develop an attachment to one or two people who will be there to respond to them. Educating new parents as to the importance of this may greatly reduce the child's feelings of anxiety and abandonment and the need to control others in the present and the future.

Care centres can ensure that while a one-to-many relationship does not replace parent attachment, it is assuring if it is a small as possible ratio, and that a staff member is constant for that child so a relationship can be built. Early childhood care and education centres should also operate in a manner that is encouraging and inclusive of grandparents through activities, openness and fostering intergenerational links. Children transfer secure primary attachment to other adults and widen their circle of trust (Ainsworth 1991). In the event of an emergency, the child will feel secure with others if the parents are absent.

When a baby is able to sit up, she will likely enjoy simple games, which, along with humour, robust action and excitement, especially from fathers, teach stress reduction, enquiry, being able to deal with the unexpected, and the fact that life is fun, not a threat (Grossman *et al.* 2002). As a child becomes more responsive, some tactile lap and finger games can be played such as 'Incy Wincy Spider' or 'Round and Round the Garden'. Bath times are great fun times for both parents to be involved with a baby, pouring water, splashing and blowing bubbles. This all helps babies to feel that they are enjoyed, and that they also have some control over their surroundings.

Try to promote the learning of 'empathic anticipatory language'. As a baby grows and begins to realize that she is a separate being she will show distress when her caregivers are out of sight. Teach the parent to consider anticipation of distress and how to be ready to provide reassurance. The parent should use the same words when leaving and returning so that the child gradually learns their connection to the return: 'I am going now but *I will come back*. See, I said *I would come back*.' The parent may reflect back to their baby any distress in the baby's voice, tone or words; for example, 'You were scared when Mummy went away.'

Children who experience such soothing behaviours, including rocking, stroking and holding, will likely be less anxious (Beebe and Lachmann 2002). Anxiety is often protected with anger.

Toddlers

Maintaining safety and care increasingly needs to be balanced with increased mobility and adventurousness for the child. Parents may require coaching to continue attachment while allowing the child the excitement of independence. They may also need to set more boundaries to manage any wilful behaviour that results from the child's developing autonomy (see pp.52–58 on boundary setting). While toddlers

enjoy doing things together with their primary caregiver, they also enjoy being able to venture away to explore alone.

Promote relationship-building activities such as:

- reading a book
- building with blocks
- drawing with crayons
- singing nursery rhymes
- playing finger games/songs such as 'There Were Ten in the Bed' or 'Twinkle Twinkle Little Star'
- walking in the garden to look for flowers, butterflies or birds
- posting small objects through a hole cut in the top of a plastic container, or rolling objects such as balls or toy cars down a slope – for example, a tray or piece of wood
- accompanied water play in a bowl or bath
- pushing and dragging the child on a tricycle or truck
- swimming lessons
- helping carry things, dig things and activities involving large motor movements.

If children have had a responsive parent play with them, they will later be able to play alone.

I, me, mine

The famous developmental psychologist Erik Erikson said that the first 18 months to two years of life are needed for the child to decide if the world is a place to be trusted (Eriksen 1963).

The activities and tasks described above encourage professional helpers and parents to foster exactly this. This is a major contribution to whether children will grow into adults who have to continually use anger to protect themselves in a world that cannot be trusted – a predisposition to 'attack first' reduces many opportunities in life for relational, occupational and material betterment. Erikson suggests that a sense of safety allows a person to better attain some level of autonomy (Eriksen 1963). Care centres and children's homes need to have boundaries, routines and relationships that provide that safety.

It is interesting to watch the patterns of movement of children around two years old in a new environment. They will venture out to explore or play with a toy and then return to their attached person and then venture out again and return again. A secure attachment to their carer will help a child to go out into the world both now and later in life.

Children will also begin to understand that some things belong to them and, unfortunately, that some things don't. This denial of control and ownership may induce strong anger and/or sadness. It is at this time that we often require children to share their belongings with other children. Tantrums may be engaged in as a physical expression of the horrible reality that the world does not revolve around them (tantrums are covered in more detail later in the book; see pp.113–119). Having a safe place to return to with this traumatic insight is important.

Adults should remember that, although a two-year-old looks more like a child than a baby, it is easy for parents and carers to begin to expect more maturity than the child actually possesses. What we may see as a tantrum may be a fear and desperation response, which requires comforting and calming.

Anna recalled that the last time two-year-old Sam visited the doctor he needed to have a painful wound dressed. She showed her understanding of Sam's fear by holding him and speaking comfortingly while at the same time focusing on Sam's new experience of listening to the doctor's stethoscope. She was careful to relate this part of their visit to Sam's father when they got home.

The world is full of choices that we make every second that we live. Limitations, eliminations and boundaries help us negotiate each day. Limiting choices at this time helps a child to develop autonomy. Offer a banana or an apple; porridge or corn flakes; the red sweatshirt or the blue sweatshirt today. Be aware, however, that we face the consequence of conflict if we swamp a small child with choices. (See 'Sara May gets dressed', a story later in this book, p.199.)

Professional helpers may need to guide parents in the need for appropriate affection, particularly if the child has an attachment disorder. An attachment disorder is usually evidenced when a child is ambivalent about parents being present, avoidant of dependency and strong displays of affection, or just chaotic or disorganized in her behaviour (Ainsworth et al. 1978, 1991; Karen 1990b). Children need to be able to make choices about important things, such as when and to whom to give affection. It is not a good idea to force a small child to kiss a relative (see the poem 'Grandpa's whiskers' on p.208). This time in a child's life is an important opportunity to develop the child's will and ability to cope with a developing selfhood. To do this she needs to experience security, love, the chance for safe discovery and exploration, and positive limit setting.

Parents sometimes need guidance to see the importance of play for development and imagination. Children at this time are developing an ability to be imaginative and creative. They begin to use symbols in their play – a block for a telephone, making engine noises as they push a toy car, a painted square for a house. While it is important that parents realize the child's increased need for language development, it is easier for a child if parents use simpler sentences at first, particularly if they are giving instructions: 'Put the book on the shelf' rather than 'Put the book on the shelf and then pick up your cars and put them in the toy box.' Parents should talk in simple sentences about what they are doing: 'I am going to put the washing on the line now'; 'Let's feed the dog.' Two-year-olds like to be constantly involved in what the parent is doing, like passing the pegs to hang out the washing and helping to put the shopping away.

Parents will be more aware of having to give constant time to their child at this stage, and professionals need to note any resistance at doing this, especially if the care centre is being used for avoidance of parental involvement.

Times like this are a valuable opportunity to increase a child's vocabulary and knowledge: 'Pass me two pegs now'; 'That's a pink peg – see, here's another pink peg'; 'Come out. Help me take the washing in.' As a child's speaking ability increases, the possibility of confused frustration decreases because the child can communicate more specifically with words. Two-year-olds can still  understand far more than they can say, however, and it is important to remember this if adults are talking in front of a small child.

At 22 months Kim was fascinated with a library book that had a picture of a child crying. 'Baba sad,' she said over and over as she looked at the picture. Her facial expression mirrored that of the child in the book as she spoke.

In the last decade professionals have become more aware of the dangerous effect of violence on the developing brain. If a young child experiences verbal or physical violence, or is constantly in an atmosphere of violence and abuse, the child may be left with greater neural sensitivity and hyper-reactivity (Fancourt 2000; Perry 1997). Family violence professionals now ensure that parents they are dealing with understand this danger to their child's future.

Tom and Anna were having couple counselling because of their ongoing physical and verbal abuse of one another. Their counsellor, sensing how much they loved their children, showed them a picture of scans of two children's brains in a book. One was the brain of a child brought up in a 'normal' home. The other was that of a child brought up experiencing violence. The difference in brain size and development was remarkable. Tom and Anna sat and looked at the picture for several moments. 'Can you photocopy that for us?' asked Tom. 'I think we need to have that on our fridge door to remind us of what we are doing.'

Because of a two-year-old's developing autonomy and immature language skills and because she does not yet understand many adult concepts, there is a great possibility for conflict at this stage. Parents should have overall control of the situation without being dictators; children need to feel that adults have that control in order to feel secure. Parents often feel insecure themselves because they sense that others are watching them and judging their ability to parent.

'I have had to start some good self talk in my head,' said Marlene. 'I tell myself. I am doing what I believe is best. Other people don't have to go home with my child and take care of her. I do.'

Those professionals supporting parents and their children need to help tune parental expectations to the level of the child's physical co-ordination.

Meal times can be a time of conflict with two-year-olds.

Remember:

- Small children spread food around and can't always get it in their mouth.
- Small children can't be expected to sit right through a meal.
- Small children can't sit quietly.
- Small children often don't want to eat as they have appropriately snacked. They need smaller, more frequent meals.
- Small children sometimes just enjoy the autonomy of a refusal to comply.
- If parents coerce children into eating they risk starting a pattern of game playing where the child vies for control; this may go on for years.

Being three

Conflict with three-year-olds is potentially reduced with the advent of more language, more concepts such as time, and better motor skills. The contrariness of 'no' is over, toilet training is possibly complete, and the child is sleeping better. The child will have developed an identification of boy or girl, and be seeking to behave according to gender-based models.

Megan was visiting the community nurse for a 'well child' check-up. Jamie would be four in just a few weeks. 'This is the time to watch out for him,' she was told. 'You think he knows all the rules and boundaries but four-year-olds push the limits.'

Megan was enjoying Jamie's more settled behaviour and found this hard to believe. Or perhaps she didn't want to believe it. Jamie knew now, for instance, that he was not to go out onto the street alone.

Two days later Megan was cooking tea. Jamie was playing happily in the back garden. Her husband Rob had gone out for a run. The phone rang. It was a friend who lived at the top of the hill.

'Did you know that Rob is out running and Jamie is running along a couple of hundred metres behind him? He's got his running shoes on just like his dad! I'm just going out now to see if I can stop him.'

Being four

Professional helpers should warn parents to brace themselves for another round of development that could include conflict and aggression by the age of four. Conflict is increasingly likely, especially for boys, who at this age get a shot of testosterone that generates activity and competition. Gender differences discovered at the age of three may be expressed by copying both the good and the not so good of the same-sex parent.

Four-year-olds seek the challenge of developing their initiative. They crave opportunities for adventure, to build, knock down and rebuild, to imagine and create, to pretend and to explore possibilities. To do this they will contest previous limits that have been set, and it may feel at times as if parents have to start all over again with the boundary patrol. The child, however, has more language ability, which now includes the ability to ask exploratory questions such as 'Why?' This is the age of the 'Little Explorer', 'Professor' or 'Scientist'.

A four-year-old called out 'Come and look at me. I'm doing something extremely dangerous!' The four-year-old was sitting on the roof of the house having climbed up the plum tree to get there. There followed a hair-raising few minutes as the child was guided carefully back to safety. Dad had said, 'Wow that's amazing – well done', while Mum had said, 'Help. How can we get him down? He's going to fall.'

Gender differences in attitudes to exploration and adventure, contrasted with the mother's concern for safety and nurture, are shown in the example above. How the parent copes with situations such as the one above will determine how the growing child approaches new situations and challenges later in life. If the parent gets angry and punishes the child, she will squash the child's future abilities to meet these challenges, and yet she needs to keep the child safe. Possible responses to the example above may be:

'I know you like to climb. It's fun and exciting but that was not a good idea because you could have been badly hurt if you had fallen. Let's go to the park where you can climb on the climbing frames or you can climb the plum tree, but don't climb onto the roof.'

'Great work! So let's do some great work getting you down. See that branch below your foot? Check to see if it can take your weight.'

There are some who have called the four-year-old stage 'The First Adolescence' (Miller 1997). In many ways children at this age face some similar challenges to those to be faced later:

- exploring roles (at this time, dressing up in Mum or Dad's clothes) and a sense of who they are
- developing initiatives to face new challenges
- becoming more involved in play
- socializing with their peer group
- pushing parental boundaries to prove to themselves that they can cope on their own.

A four-year-old is usually attending an early childhood centre and looking forward with excitement and trepidation to starting school.

She has a growing ability to think and reason. A four-year-old can grasp the idea that Mum or Dad can be mean and angry but still be the same person who is caring and loving, and who the child in turn loves and admires. It may be hard, however, to cope with knowing that Mum and Dad have a relationship from which the child is at times excluded, and feelings of jealousy may arise.

It may be hard to know that Mum and Dad continue to live their life when the child is not present. If the parent thinks of jealousy, in this case as fear – fear of loss – it can make it easier to understand some four-year-old tantrums and how the parent might deal with them. How the parent helps a four-year-old cope with such situations will greatly influence the way the child will deal with such situations later in life.

When one four-year-old was left at nursery she demanded to know what Mum or Dad would be doing that day. If the reply was, 'Oh just boring old work or just housework,' the four-year-old would settle happily down to play.

Four-year-olds have difficulty distinguishing between fact and fantasy, which may explain their enjoyment of fanciful fairy stories at this time. Such stories with witches, wizards, evil stepmothers or giants are often a metaphor of the child's world, where her powerful giant parents appear to have magical powers to control and can still change again to become a fairy godmother or a benevolent king.

Zara had enjoyed the story of *Red Riding Hood* but when she found out about her mother's pregnancy she hid the book on the top shelf in her room and made her parents promise not to read it. Some sensitive enquiry from her parents led them to discover that Zara believed that in order for the baby to be born her mother would have to be cut open with an axe as the wolf in the story had been.

Four-year-old boys may be seen as more difficult in nursery. They are more likely to engage in robust play, stress equipment to breaking point, compete, make up guns, wrestle, be noisier, take on superhero persona and challenge rules. Professionals can often be heard to say, 'They are ready for school' and wish them gone. It is likely that they are dealing with the second largest burst of testosterone that they will ever have. This is wonderful boy life and the challenge is to use the energy wisely and to channel it. Rather than inhibit play and repress them, ensure that there is equipment available for them to use (for more on play, see pp.27–30). Invite them to wrestle on gym mats under supervision, following good simple rules. Put language to the superhero stories. Issue gun licences, enjoy the noise, and make sure that there is outdoor space. Hold boundaries firmly and ask men into the centre to talk about anything from tools to reading a boy book.

Any tantrums that ensue may have a wider source of causes:

- competing and losing
- anxiety about leaving day care/the early education centre
- the need for strong physical expression due to hormones (boys)
- intolerance from women/mothers who don't understand 'boy energy'
- fear of loss, rejection
- being thought too little to cope.

It is important that a parent helps the children to talk about their fears, and it is important that boundaries are held, especially for boys, due to the search for order and security they are experiencing. (Professional helpers are invited to look at Chapter 9 on parenting troubles for parents of preschoolers.)

So the role of parents and parenting is fundamental, and may lie behind a child's angry behaviour. For the time being, we keep the main point of focus on the child and the child's experiences.

Chapter 2

The Lives of Children

How They Experience the World and How It Impacts on Them

This chapter covers some of the important aspects of children's experiences of the world around them as they start to grow, how they make sense of them – and how their experiences can create angry feelings if the adults caring for them do not consider their experiences.

The importance of play

Play presents a setting for social exchange, conflict and problem solving. It is fun and releases anxiety, energy and creativity. Many parents seem to have accepted, however, that:

- our learning begins when we go to school
- we only learn through the education system
- work is superior to play.

All of these are incorrect! Parents and even childcare workers may need reminding that play is expressive, stress reducing, and a way of learning. Assisting parents, childminders and foster carers in remembering the value of play is important.

Let us look at the three fallacies in more detail.

Our learning begins when we go to school

This is not true. Learning begins when we are born. In fact, we learn more that will equip us for life before we go to school than all the learning that happens after. Some of the learning is: to speak, to use the language that we will use for our whole life, to walk, to put things together and pull them apart, to stand up for ourselves, to fit into social systems, to relate and interact with others, that we are worthwhile, and to develop the core self-esteem needed for the rest of our life, how cars, shops, television, roads, buildings and the weather work, how to laugh and smile and win people over, to discipline our bodies and impulses, to use our bodies to play games, sport and to perform tasks, to obey orders and learn when not to obey, to learn right from wrong, to express emotions, empathy for others, gender identity and roles, to draw and express with our hands, to use tools, colour and music, the power of connection with others, and how to eat and sit and 'behave'.

Play is one way that we learn. Our bodies learn, our minds learn and our emotions learn. Some people don't have the opportunity to learn in this manner, however, and they are hampered for parts of their lives until they do. If a company manager is unable to empathize with others, then he will need to learn this quickly or he will be unable to work with his staff and someone else may soon take his place. Play, interacting with others, and loving and being loved are the three ways we gather the most important learning of our life, and this happens before we get to school. After that we are just adding to the base laid down in early years.

We only learn through the education system

Not true. Education systems tend to be geared to the learning and recording of facts, although the primary school years place more emphasis on creativity, expression and imagination. This decreases as children progress through the education system, which was initially designed on a factory model to develop skills required for the business world. Although this is important, it often ends up missing out issues such as successful relationships, happiness, creativity, using initiative, emotional literacy, co-operation and independence, and play is one of the best ways of learning these skills. When you see children playing, don't think, 'they are *just* playing', think 'they are *learning* from life'.

Work is superior to play

Not true. Schoolwork is the 'work' that many think of for children. Learning concepts and facts is important, but unless they have direct meaning and relevance to life, they have little use. When was the last time that you used calculus or trigonometry? Was it as recently as you had to use negotiation, anger management, persuasion or planning skills? Play that develops with achievement and interest gives us experience, development and enjoyment.

Perhaps it is easier to accept if we swap the word 'play' with the word 'experience'. Giving our children the greatest number and quality of experiences is the best preparation for later life.

Some of the types of play that are beneficial are as follows:

- large motor movements, such as tree climbing, kicking a ball, washing the car, batting, throwing and bowling, dancing and painting
- small motor movements, such as drawing, cutting, writing, building blocks, pick-up-sticks
- role-play, such as dressing up, doing the voices of others, playing mothers and fathers, being doctors and pilots and digger drivers, monsters, models and idols
- expressive play, such as messy play with clay, dirt, mud, playdough, cooking, fingerpaint
- sport, such as learning rules and boundaries, teamwork, losing and winning, emotional management, physical expression, physical skills, empathy, fairness.

Having fun is great. It releases fear, anger and stress. It channels energy. It stimulates creativity and sets imagination working. Play encourages real-life learning, thinking on the spot, co-operating with others, learning how to express yourself, taking the initiative, how to get what you want in balance with others' needs, following your interests, and it gives experience on which to hang other types of more formal learning.

Play helps a young child express anger and it means that in the long run the child will have less need to resort to anger because he has learned to deal with life and to respond powerfully with choices.

Usually parents and/or carers need to practise the above more than the children they are trying to 'make useful'.

Positive play: taking turns and co-operating

Given a secure and fair environment children learn to take turns with others. To help this process along we can begin playing simple games, even with a toddler, that encourage taking turns. Make a tower with blocks: 'I put on a block. Now you put on a block.' Thread cotton reels or large beads onto a string: 'You put on a bead. I put on a bead.'

As children get older, more complex games such as 'Pairs' or 'Memory' can be played with 'Snap' cards, and playing 'Snap' is another simple, effective game. Later, children can play board games. Board games help children to follow rules, take turns, learn to cope with disappointment, develop maths and language skills and experience achievement.

Play provides a setting to test autonomy and difference. A two-year-old may resist taking turns because it is normal for them to be oppositional. It may help to keep a timer in your centre or playroom so that the timer gets the blame for any boundary enforcement.

Play presents a method of working out frustrations, engaging in co-operation and conflict, expressing anger, strategizing, experiencing powerlessness in a social setting, solving problems, listening to the anger of others, and helping others to work through anger to solve their own problems.

Angry or disruptive children often withdraw empathy from others and are protecting themselves. It is therapeutic, after reducing causal factors, to engage such children back into sharing and collaboration. Early learning environments can be therapeutic in their ability to supply those opportunities.

Boys and girls: gender differences and emotional life

Children are aware of their own gender, and it affects how they experience and interact with the world around them, yet many professionals have had training based on the presupposition that there is no difference between the genders.

Boys and girls are different, and their differences have implications for understanding anger. Even at the early childhood stage gender roles are clear – due to both genetics and social conditioning we are different at birth, and continue to be different for life.

Until about seven weeks in the uterus the foetus is visibly neither boy nor girl. Around seven weeks, if it is a boy, there is a burst of testosterone that starts the development of male genitals and also differences in brain development. The boy brain has fewer connectors between hemispheres and processes different functions in different parts of the brain and in different ways to girls. An example is the greater ability of girls to process language to the extent that girls at all ages and in all cultures have better verbal skills. Male language is likely to be more kinaesthetic – males are more inclined to communicate with their bodies or action than females where the preference is verbal (Biddulph 1995, 2003; Gurian 2002). We can surmise that the expression of frustration and anger will also be expressed more kinaesthetically in boys.

Gender is the social construction that genetic sex differences are fitted into for the functioning of the culture. There is a clear point at which a child becomes more aware of who they are and how they might express their genetic difference. At about the age of three the young child finds out that he or she is either male or female. Girls realize that 'I've got one of these so I am like her and I am called a girl.' And boys realize 'I've got one of these so I am like him and I am called a boy.'

It can be problematic if there is no one there to identify with at this point – it is like growing into an empty space or defining yourself as what-you-are-not rather than something positive that you are. This could cause problems and conflict later – where possible, keep both genders around in both parenting and education environments and ensure good stories and opinions about both genders.

The major role difference that boys and girls take on is still the nurturer role for girls and the protector role for boys. Genetically, on average, boys are likely to have 30 per cent more muscle tissue than girls and so are stronger and quite reasonably expected to be the ones who are better at defending and protecting. Testosterone too, as the male hormone, assists focus, aggression, body development, brain processing and power dynamics, all of which contribute to the protector role (Biddulph 2008).

Research shows that even as babies we handle boy babies more roughly, hold them for less time, have less eye contact and speak less to them (Biddulph 2008; Sidorowicz and Lunney 1980). We do more talking with girls and this generally adds to a predisposition in relationship and nurture skills and interpersonal understanding. We generally encourage boys to be tougher, rougher and able to protect women, children and families. Such training can be seen as a layer of social conditioning over a genetic advantage for these separate roles, and this has been key to the survival of the human species, as it is with most species.

The protector role has both advantages and disadvantages for males. We are more likely to say to a three-year-old boy who has fallen and grazed himself: 'What a brave boy' or 'Be strong' or 'That didn't hurt did it?' For a girl we are more likely to say, 'That must have hurt' or 'Let me give you a cuddle' or 'Let's go and put a plaster on that.' Boys at a young age are conditioned for denial of pain and fear, and are encouraged to 'stick up for themselves'. A boy who is being bullied is likely to be encouraged and shown how to stand up for himself. A girl is more likely to be defended by a parent.

How does the protector role relate to anger?

The result of having the role of 'protector' is that it becomes unwise to show vulnerability and weakness in the world. The people you may have to be guarded against might see vulnerability and take advantage of it, and the people you are defending might see that you are not up to the job, and lose respect for you. This is so core to our relationships that we normally don't notice it, but basically, in heterosexual couples, the male is expected to be prepared to die for the female if needs be. If there is an intruder, for example, it is generally the male who is expected to front up and risk a confrontation and conflict. And if a woman is accosted, it is her male partner who is expected to go into battle for her, regardless of the odds, to minimize danger to her.

Boys will generally try to look tough and handsome to attract girls, and girls will seek males who have the strength and who don't look emotionally or physically weak. Despite decades of gender deconstruction and media challenge, the attractiveness of a male body is still based on a strong musculature, and the attractiveness of a female is based on beauty and subtle curves. This means, generally speaking, that men are conditioned to have fewer chances to express or process their vulnerable emotions such as hurt, sadness, fear, love or worry. In fact, they generally repress nearly all emotions to some extent except anger, because anger is the one empowering emotion that allows them to fight back and protect. Girls, on the other hand, are generally able to express all emotions except anger, although this is now changing.

We have a social contract, then, where the emotions are shared out rather unequally based on genetic aptitude to perform key survival tasks. This is all a generalisation, however, and there will always be people who thankfully run counter to the generalisation, but it is the main reason why about 90 per cent of the reported 'problems with anger' in young children concern boys (Pudney

2002). Unfortunately, as part of their training for life, we offer boys less empathy and care than we do to girls and women. We punish and hit them more, we shame their weakness, and we listen less to their difficulties. Consequently, boys are trained to express vulnerable emotions less and revert to angry responses more.

Given that we encourage boys to be able to access their defence and protection skills, and that anger is the emotion that best equips us to do that, we expect a boy to show anger, and to some degree we tolerate him doing that. Anger enables the narrowing of peripheral vision in order to focus on crisis and conflict, and adrenalin rushes assist the ability to combat or deal with issues in crisis mode. A neurological predisposition to 'linear problem solution' channels anger into efficient and focused conflict (Gurian 2002; Gurian and Stevens 2005; James 2007; Sax 2006).

Anger works not just for boys but also for others whom they protect. While this often means boys are first to a conflict, it may also be a problem for girls if they are doing the reverse – repressing anger and internalizing the problem. A consequence of this division is the problem boys have of repressing vulnerability, and this has major implications for male health. It also means that males will be represented at rates of about 90 per cent in aggressive behaviour such as armed combat and gang fights, in institutions such as jails and behaviour modification units in schools, and as victims in accident and emergency centres (Biddulph 2002). Professionals must find ways through to assist boys' expression of vulnerability.

Tackling gender stereotypes

Carers, educators, psychological assistants and parents, without denying the useful function of protection, should equalize things a little more to generate better lifestyles for both boys and girls. The following are suggestions that they might choose to give attention to:

- Listen to both boys and girls equally, and their problems.
- Teach problem solving (rather than rescuing), especially to girls.
- Individually protect children and investigate their concerns.
- Make it okay for boys to express sadness, hurt, pain, sickness, love, caring or fear. Encourage fathers to show the more vulnerable emotions to their children (at a moment when the child is feeling secure).
- Do not tell boys to 'Look after your mother.' It is unfair and denies a child his childhood.
- Help girls express their anger openly and directly. Get alongside a girl who is withdrawn or depressed. She may be 'sitting on' anger.
- Don't teach boys to 'fight back' as a first option.

- The way of the modern world is to use language. Talk with boys. Assist them to talk.

- Teach boys how to ask for things (asking is part of admitting and assisting their vulnerability).

- Teach boys negotiation and verbal self-defence.

- Teach children to have a plan about how to put things right, even little things.

- Teach time out and model it.

- Boys appreciate when you keep good limits and boundaries and are very consistent. Be fair in your decisions and sharing.

- Watch for patterns of 'making a child the bad one' or labelling him the 'difficult one'.

- Be positive and notice the good things about boys, especially their robust play and noise. Compliment boys as we are often verbally hard on them.

- Go outside with boys and engage in large motor movement play.

- Give children language for emotions. Use emotional words. Show authentic emotions and expressions to go with the words. Don't 'act nice' when it's not nice. It's confusing to young children who are learning life skills in emotional literacy.

- Make up 'okay' swear words (see the section on swear words on pp.119–121).

- Generate conversation on angry experiences without judging the emotion.

- Listen to anger without flinching, and appreciate the good reason behind it.

Children and society

James Gilligan, in his book *Preventing Violence* (Gilligan 2001), reports that it is shame, humiliation and disrespect in childhood and beyond that drives a person to extreme violence:

> The more a person is shamed by others, from childhood, by parents or peers who ridicule or reject him, the more he is likely to feel chronically shamed, and hypersensitive to feelings and experiences of being shamed, sometimes to the point of feeling that others are treating him with contempt or disdain, even when they are not. For such people, and they are the rule among the violent, even a minor sign of real or imagined disrespect can trigger a homicidal reaction. (Gilligan 2001, p.35)

Throughout this book we indicate ways that parents or caregivers can treat children with love, understanding, kindness, security and respect, and reduce the chance of shame that produces such destructive defences.

Unfortunately, our society does not always contribute with kindness, security and understanding to the welfare of children and families. Rather, we are dealing with a culture of shaming and guilt, with shopping malls, television channels, corporations, advertisers, billboards and even our neighbours and courts controlling people through shame and guilt. Consumerism and advertising is based on convincing the public that they are inadequate and not likeable unless they have the product being promoted.

Even seven- and eight-year-old children are now being marketed to as fair game for corporate profit. The Australian Institute coined the phrase 'corporate paedophilia' to name the publicly condoned exploitation of children (Rush and La Nauze 2006), where children are used for profit through the marketing of sexualized goods. Children are also taught to feel shame if they do not have certain brands of shoes, clothing and paraphernalia, just as parents are made to feel ashamed if they live in certain neighbourhoods. Shame is then covered with anger and violent behaviour, towards either themselves or others (Nathanson 1992).

Since the 1980s the gap between rich and poor has widened worldwide. Many children are growing up in extreme poverty in a land of plenty. Gilligan (2001) and other social commentators have provided evidence to suggest that it is in countries where this financial discrepancy is the greatest that there is the highest level of violent crime (Wilkinson and Pickett 2009). If we want to live in a violence-free community, a much fairer distribution of resources is needed, together with a greater sense of care for others beyond ourselves. We need to pick up the deficits that some children should not need to bear. A society's children belong to everyone, and they need the proverbial village to look after them.

The effects of violence on children

Witnessing violence can have serious, long-lasting effects on children, as discussed briefly in Chapter 1. It is now known that the brain development of such children can be seriously affected, particularly those parts of the brain concerned with the regulation of emotions (Fancourt 2000; Frodl *et al.* 2010; Hoskins, Roth and Giancola 2010). This leaves a child, and later an adult, struggling to cope with, and manage, anger and anxiety.

Robyn Fancourt, in her book *Brainy Babies* (2000, p.149), states:

> Neglect or abuse can impair or destroy the development of the brain leading to disastrous results for children. These range from those children who can neither tolerate nor learn from normal daily stress to those whose early life experiences leave a legacy of anti-social or self-destructive behaviour.

Abused children living in violent or chaotic homes are unable to learn, lack social skills, and are at risk of developing other damaging behaviour with lifelong consequences. This has been widely documented in children who witness or hear such violence between their parents without any personal physical injury.

Witnessing violence, even if it is not done directly to them, is terrifying for children. This is particularly so if the person being hurt is a mother or father on whom the child is dependent for care, love and survival. A child will fear the loss of this person. The violence the child watches stays with him in his mind and is often replayed in his interactions with other children. For those who witness violence there is also the question 'When will that happen to me?'

If a child is traumatized by what he sees he will find ways of coping with this. Some children will react very violently to seemingly non-threatening events because they have become so hyper-vigilant and because they are unable to moderate their feelings. Other children will 'switch off' or dissociate. For such children relationships and schoolwork become difficult. They are unable to stay focused in the present and have difficulty concentrating.

Television, videos, films and computer games bombard children with violent images. Small children have difficulty distinguishing between fact and fantasy. Adults may say to themselves, 'This is just acting.' A small child may not. If we want secure children who are able to function well socially and go on to successfully raise secure children themselves we must ensure that children live free of violence. If a child does experience a chaotic and/or violent home life, we must ensure that suitable treatment is available to the child as soon as possible, as well as to the parents.

We suggest:

- An ongoing public education programme about the effects of violence on children and sources of help. This should be given on television, radio, billboards and in newspapers.

- Increased support and learning for parents through education programmes and increased child health provision, including home visits by health professionals. This assistance should be of a positive nature so that parents will then seek help rather than fear that their children will be taken from them.

- Support for parents who undertake parental education, such as time off work or free courses.

- Compulsory attendance at parenting courses for those involved in family violence.

- Providing information to parents through doctors and midwives during pregnancy about the effects of violence on children and the need for a secure, loving environment. This may need to be spelt out clearly for those who do not know how to give a child a secure home because they have not known such an environment themselves.

- Assistance with therapy costs for those who have experienced violence as children so that they do not pass on similar experiences to their own children.

- Therapy for children who have witnessed violence at home.

- Laws should be passed that protect children from violence.

- The violent content of television programmes should be significantly reduced, particularly during peak viewing times.

Consideration also needs to be given to:

- What are good bed times for children that avoid television violence?

- What sorts of trailers are being shown for adult programmes during children's viewing?

- What sort of violence and poor conflict models are being shown in cartoons that children can watch?

- A tax on violent incidents in television and film productions to restrict violent incidents and to fund solutions to the problems caused by modelled violence.

- Early help and support in families where children are consistently demonstrating aggressive, self-harming and/or disruptive behaviour.

The cost of these provisions would be covered in the long term by a reduction in the costs of violent crime. Children tend to reflect the environment that they experience while growing up. As a society we have a responsibility to limit and regulate the use of violence in the media, eliminate violence in our homes and provide services that support these ideals. As parents and advising professionals we are responsible for ensuring our own behaviour is positive and educative of others who, nearly always, actually want the best for their children. And the best place to start when changing violence in our community is with young children.

Chapter 3

Skills for Caring for the Angry Child

Empathy

Empathy is the reason why people choose to be professional helpers. They have chosen to care enough to extend empathy for others and then show a desire to help them. Many parents and even some helpers have limited empathy, and this restricts them in their work. Lack of empathy is a key reason for a child or an adult to feel angry and to stay angry. Anger protects a person from injustice, which, by definition, is unempathic. Listening empathically reduces anger. Fostering empathy in relationships not only increases kindness, trust and happiness, but it also reduces anxiety, anger and the bad choices that sometimes follow those feelings.

The following description should attune us to the importance of empathy and particularly the need for children to have empathic adults around them, especially if they are preverbal or have a limited vocabulary.

Empathy is the key to successful relationships, with everyone the child comes into contact with in her life now and in the future, everyone that parents or caregivers come into contact with, including toddlers, and everyone else in the house or workplace. It is a critical factor in people splitting up relationships, getting promotions, being happy, being understood, fitting into a family or a community. It is the key to the end of wars on Earth!

Empathy will take children further in life than an expensive education or lots of money. It is the ability to imagine sitting inside someone else's skin, their life, their mind, their experience, their problem, their age, their gender or their culture, and to imagine, as accurately as we can, how it is to be them. It requires being able to gather enough information to guess accurately how they feel, and think, and even how they see you.

It you have empathized with them accurately you have left yourself for a moment and joined them. In that moment of joining with them you have become them and you have a relationship. This means that you cannot hurt them because in that moment you are them and you would be hurting yourself.

Competition tends to encourage a reduction of empathy. If you are competing with someone, especially if there is only one prize or one winner, then you need to withdraw empathy and focus instead on yourself. You withdraw from the other's feelings of disappointment and centre only on your own feelings. Business competition and competition for social status can be ruthless de-empathizers. Conflict resolution and restorative justice practitioners endeavour to 're-empathize' relationships, to heal feelings, and to produce win–win rather than 'de-empathized', win–lose outcomes.

Empathy is an essential quality of being a helping professional or a parent. You cannot bring up children without it. Children are fortunately very much entrusted to a parent's care and power, so it becomes easier for parents to risk developing empathy for their children. Children are also less likely to hurt a parent back due to their dependency.

Some people start parenting practice on animals as, like young children, they have little power and are unlikely to hurt us. Most adults find very small children and young animals entrancing and easy to adore. Possibly we are unconsciously reminded of our own perfect, helpless selves in our early years. Innocence and large eyes encourage us to be empathic towards children and so to give money to charity or to buy consumer goods marketed with childlike images. Childish innocence is a way through defended hearts.

Some people have been hurt so much that they have a problem risking empathy with others. They feel that they need all their energy to focus on protecting their own needs. They may then treat people as objects in order to protect themselves. This creates a life empty of close relationships or, at a minimum, full of distant relationships that don't seem to get any closer.

If a person had little empathy as a child then they may have some difficulty with parenting (Hendrix 1990; Karen 1990a), but it is essential that a person develops empathy so that their own children can develop inter-relational empathy for their own lives. Many parents heal their own childhood by opening deep empathy for their children. They may, however, only risk empathy with people that they have complete power over. This can go both ways – it can work to increase empathy and trust, or it can, when under stress, revert to replication of some of the neglect that they experienced as children (Hendrix 1988; Karen 1998). Professional helpers should monitor parents who have experienced such a lack of empathy as children.

Prisoners in jail often rehabilitate by risking empathy for their own small children as a starting place. Adults who have Asperger syndrome or autism usually have trouble with immediate empathy and will need some form of assistance to more deliberately recognize expressions and actions, and learn what they can mean from memory. Their families often report struggling with their lack of empathic responsiveness and connection.

Empathy is an essential quality of being a parental figure. A child cannot develop empathy unless they learn it from a parent or carer in their lived relationship. The best place to learn how to have an empathic relationship is from the first caregiver, through care and response.

How do you get an empathic child? You get an empathic child not by trying to teach the child and admonish the child to be empathic; you get an empathic child by being empathic with the child. The child's understanding of relationships can only be from the relationships he's experienced. (Sroufe 1989, from a talk at the City University of New York, Graduate Centre, quoted in Karen 1998, p.195)

Exercise: Understanding the child's world

Try the following exercise or read it for a parent. Ask the parent to give additional empathic responses for each line:

- Imagine yourself as a three-year-old child. What would your body feel like?

- What would it be like to be so clumsy with your little hand when you go to the toilet?

- What would it be like to try to skip and fall over because you hadn't got the co-ordination?

- Imagine yourself being dropped off at a strange caregiver/babysitter's place and your parents were running late and left you all alone without even a hug or kiss...and nothing was familiar.

- Imagine being unable to get your small penis out of the front of your underpants and becoming more anxious as you needed to pee.

- Imagine what it would be like to be ignored by a group of happy, chatting adults when you couldn't get your voice heard above their knees.

- Imagine yourself having strange people leaning over your cot and not even having clear focus to see them.

- Imagine not being able to see people's eyes unless they were sitting down or bending over.

- Imagine the rising panic in you as you walked through the house looking for your mum and couldn't find her. Room after room, the fear and sense of betrayal and abandonment increases. Stand in the utter loneliness. Then hear Mum's call from the toilet and run to the toilet door and bang angrily on it and then slump in a heap and cry. Why did you bang angrily?

- Imagine a teacher telling you to come now to sit on the mat when you were right in the middle of the most exciting construction you have ever made and it's not finished.

- Imagine the most comforting thing alive was a tone of voice saying noises that meant nothing but familiarity.

- Imagine getting into trouble in the bathroom because you let the door shut and you can't reach the handle and it's cold and you may stay there forever and die there.

Talk with the parent who has just done this exercise with you about ways in which they could understand the infant world better. Being able to continually put ourselves into a child's skin and mind allows the child to feel close and to build a relationship. It also equips a child to be able to do this with others. It is the basis of kindness and compassion.

It is impossible to bully someone if you think what it would feel like to be bullied. The bully has no empathy and is living in that moment totally in her own existence and from a position of survival. Parents and children need some training to stop and to step into someone else's position. Even employers should do this if their staff are to function at their best.

There is a requirement first that we be able to experience and name feelings ourselves. If life has been hard and feelings have frightened us, we may have shut them down in order to cope. We may need the help of a counsellor or psychotherapist to access our feelings, to name them, and to make sense of them and communicate them. These personal, relational skills need to be modelled to children.

As parents and carers we have a responsibility to provide our children with emotional language and expressive cues. We do this by tuning into how our child might be feeling, and reflecting those feelings back with words and facial expressions. 'He took your truck and now you are very, very angry?' We can't be sure that we are right and really know how another feels so it helps to add a questioning tone. That way a child can say 'No' or 'Yes.' We then assist the child to accurately give language to their experience.

Julie talks about her lonely childhood with parents who were 'always stoned': 'They just weren't there,' she says. 'It was like there was a screen down in front of them that shut them off from us.' Julie struggled to cope with this early experience of abandonment. She never learnt to feel that the important adults in her life were present and she found it hard to be 'there' for her children.

The following exercises may help:

- Turn on the television without sound. Actors often exaggerate emotions, especially in soap operas. Write or call out the emotion each actor is portraying.

- Sit in a shopping mall for a few minutes and watch people going by. What are the clues about how individual people are feeling?

- Spend time observing your child at home and doing the same as you did in the shopping mall.

- Deliberately show emotions such as joy, excitement, pride and contentment to your baby or toddler. This is educating a child to express and communicate feelings in a manner that is in response to a trusted person and thus the baby or toddler learns to bond and relate.

Listen for phrases that indicate a parent or educator has empathy. Their language will have phrases like these if they are empathizing with the child:

'Let me help you put your jacket on. It will be cold where we are going.'

'Did something frighten you? That's awful. Daddy hates being frightened too; let me hug you and help you feel safe.'

'Standing and going out the front of your class to talk sounds really scary.'

'It's really hard waiting for a biscuit when you really want one.'

'It must really be uncomfortable having all that poo between your legs.'

'Are you feeling angry with me for leaving you with Nana?'

'It must be hard having to walk and stand for such a long time shopping.'

'Did the big dog scare you when it licked your face?'

A child will have phrases like these if they are developing empathy for others:

'Can I have a biscuit when you have finished Mum?' (empathy for Mum)

'Mummy, I think that we need to give baby hugs. She's crying.' (empathy for baby)

'Mandy [doll] is upset because she has to go to the doctor's.' (empathy for Mandy is really empathy for self)

'Don't take my train. You wouldn't like it if I took yours.' (teaching empathy to a peer)

'Your mum sounds unhappy.' (empathy for lesser known acquaintance)

'Quick. Come and help Michael. He's fallen over and is crying.' (empathy for hurt child)

The exercise of constantly imagining what it is like to be the other person is a basic tool of life. We gift it to our children by doing it with them.

Helping professionals or parents who are able to continually put themselves into a child's skin and mind allows the child to feel close and to build a relationship with them. It also teaches a child to do this with others. It is impossible to bully someone if you are feeling what it would be like to be bullied.

Empathy and assumptions

We cannot be sure that we know what other people are feeling and thinking and therefore that our empathy is matched. We need to check out that we are imagining it right. This is particularly so with little children who have much less language to inform us with. The younger the child, the more we have to guess because there is less information. As toddlers get more language, we need to be constantly asking if we have got our guesses right. Apart from building relationships, checking assumptions is empowering for the child who becomes defined as the authority on what they feel and what is going on. Many adults come to counselling and therapy having had childhoods and even adulthoods of being told what they feel and believe.

Professionals can help parents with empathy development through developing awareness of the perspectives of others, and parents can then do the same with their children.

Simply:

- Coach the parent to increase the imagination of what might be happening to feelings, beliefs and perceptions of situations as they might be held or experienced by the child. Encourage the parent to make these assumptions overt to the professional. Some of these may be wild guesses and some will be a clear reality for the child.

- The parent should then check the assumptions against the professional's own assumptions and explain why they have made them. The professional should also question why the parent made that guess, based on what clues and indicators. Clues come from facial expressions, body language, action, words and gut connection. These are the basis of the 'good guessing'. The professional should then add her reasons and data that are also good guesses.

- The professional should then ask the parent and coach them in the forming of good questions that can be used to ask and check. Are they clean of impositions? For example, the question, 'Are you unhappy because you can't clean up your toys?' is imposing the parent's agenda rather than being empathic. A better question might be, 'Are you angry because you were having fun building that tower and I told you to stop?' Are the questions respectful? For example, a response from the child of 'But I already told you that' is an offended response. Offended responses increase anger rather than decrease it.

- The parent should go away and immediately test the 'good guesses' to see if they match the child's experience.

- Parents need to consciously give themselves credit every time they get it right as a way of bringing consciousness to what they don't know. A good activity is for an adult to do the exercise with another intimate adult or partner.

'Good guessing' and checking builds respect and intimacy. Apart from allowing us to get past our assumptions, it sometimes helps the other person put words to their experience. Young children need those words, and handing them a phrase can be an enormous relief, reducing the need for physical expression and even tantrums. Giving a voice to those who do not have one is an act of empathic support.

Discussions between nurses/baby professionals and parents often have to be a collaboration of creating a voice for a baby. The parent comes with data based on guesses and assumptions. This is combined with the greater experience of the professional, and a consensus or possibility list is generated for testing. The greatest moment of despair in a parent's life is, of course, the moment when the collaboration does not supply the good guess, and a baby continues to be distressed. For preverbal infants, our wisdom is their language.

Parents who had little attachment themselves as under-fives will have more difficulty with attachment and empathy with their own children (Karen 1998; Main and Weston 1981). This can be learned, often slowly, and may be the task of professionals. Childcare centres should check an employee's ability to empathize before employing them, or commit to training in this most essential element to childcare.

A colleague of mine who is now a trainer identifies himself somewhere on the autism spectrum. He relates that after a marriage collapse and loss of his family, partly due to his lack of ability to relate empathically, he sat down with the classic page of facial expressions and learned them along with the feeling words that match them. Next he learned the body language that went with them. He learned and practised them rigorously over years. He now works empathically with emotional issues in groups with considerable expertise. He works cognitively through clues rather than kinaesthetically through 'gut' recognitions and 'feeling connections'.

Accepting emotions

Empathy allows us to accept emotions, whether they are negative or positive, and therefore not to shame or criticize children for their feelings. What they feel is neither right nor wrong, it just is how it is, and true empathy accepts that and validates the feeling and thus the child. The parent or professional may not agree with the reason or perception that generated the feeling, but even that empathically generates a will to understand haw those thoughts were so.

Neither does empathizing with the feeling mean that *you* would feel that way in that situation. You don't have to agree with the child's opinion, but you do need to accept their feelings and how the child got that opinion, because that is the reality of that child's experience, feeling and thinking. Getting inside the experience of others with unconditional acceptance is the core of trusting relationships.

Natalie, an early childhood educator, finds Rebecca, a three-year-old, hiding in the centre washroom. She refuses to come to 'mat time'. Natalie takes her hand and tries to lead her out. Rebecca screams and bites Natalie's hand. Natalie has an immediate response of yelling at Rebecca. A colleague comes in and sees the drama: one frightened and angry child and one hurt and angry teacher. Within seconds she empathizes with the anger at the bite mark and suggests that Natalie cools off outside – 'That must have hurt!' Then she empathizes with the child who, it turns out, is frightened of a visitor who has come to speak to the children. The child's reason is not adult and informed, but it is valid for the child. The visitor is from the fire service and wants to talk to the children about fire safety. By empathizing with the child, Melissa understands that the uniform is probably frightening and may even have a past negative association. Both Natalie and Rebecca have good reasons for feeling angry and for the feeling needing to be validated.

Failure to understand, failure to accept the child's reality and feelings, incorrect interpretations, impositions of what you think they *should* feel and think are frustrating and disempowering for the child. The disempowerment of being misunderstood is food for just anger. Continued lack of empathy generates despair and fury.

Empathize with the feeling, validate it, discover the thinking (reasons) behind it, create safety, and modify the reasons if they are clearly inaccurate.

Basic communication

The task is to teach the child in those five, short, early years the skills of communication and relating that will support them for life. Additionally, caring for children under five, either as a parent, day care worker or educator, requires considerable effort on behalf of the adult to decode the child's needs and emotions and to assist the child to express herself accurately while she is in the learning process. A major reason for frustration and anger is an inability to express and communicate oneself clearly.

If caregivers or parents are able to show children that they are trying to understand how the child is feeling, then children feel less alone with powerful, often scary, emotions, and learn that they can ask for support and assistance. Poorly attached children sometimes get credit for their 'independence', but this can lead to isolated and mistrusting lives. Children who experience nurture and help around strong emotions are able to be handle relationship intimacy and aloneness, and know that they can ask and get help throughout life. They have a greater ability to handle anger, grief, hurt or fear without feeling overwhelmed and becoming further isolated.

By the time Simon was four he had learned to go to his room if he was very angry and throw his soft toys at a floor cushion in the corner of the room. His mother soon realized that if she knocked on the door and peeped in and said, 'It sounds like you are really wild about something?' Simon would stop yelling and throwing things and tell her what was wrong and then he would be calm again.

An anger vocabulary

Developing a vocabulary is the first stage of taking kinaesthetic expression, using noises such as roars and crying, and putting them into words that greatly sharpen the meaning of the communication. If children have a vocabulary for their feelings, they do not need to act them out to the same extent.

Everyone needs at least ten words that describe degrees and qualities of anger, and so allow accurate communication with others at moments of discomfort. Many professionals need to check that they have that many. Here are some possible words for feeling angry.

Mildly angry	Angry	Very angry
Irritated	Mad	Furious
Grumpy	Irate	Raging
Huffy	Exasperated	Berserk
Indignant	Upset	Inflamed
Annoyed	Resentful	Incensed
Frustrated	Cross	Wild
Niggled	Agitated	Livid

Some of these words may seem too hard for a young child, but children are capable of extraordinary vocabulary if supported by an adult. The key to young children using anger vocabulary is getting their familiar adults to use more words.

A child became fascinated with the word 'soporific' after hearing it in a Beatrix Potter storybook. The adult read it and explained it. For a long time after that she would say when she was tired 'I'm feeling very soporific.' The *sound* of words often makes them attractive, not their common usage or shortness.

Listening

Listening is underdone and underrated. We estimate that quality listening can dissipate about 80 per cent of anger. It costs nothing but a few moments' time, and nearly all adults are capable of it. It is a poor comment on our society that some have to pay a lot of money for someone to listen to them.

Claudia taught nine-year-olds at a primary school. It seemed that for years she got some of the more needy children and so had to deal with more behavioural problems and that was hard work. She had been to the principal several times and asked for assistance. It felt to her like she never got help or understanding. The current class was 'dragging her down' and it seemed unfair that she had so many problems while, in her eyes, others got better deals. After long consideration, one night, she wrote her resignation and put it in an envelope. At the appointment the next day she launched into the principal with considerable anger about the problems, his lack of care, her lack of energy for the class, and she banged the resignation on his desk. He listened to the outpouring and was not reactive but showed signs of really entering into empathy and understanding with where she was coming from. Slowly the rage turned to tears and she stopped. The principal's listening had been so genuine, focused, and empathic that she paused in silence, then picked up the letter and walked out. Fifteen minutes of genuine listening and empathy had changed weeks of stewing anger. Although he had promised nothing, the principal did give her more support.

Partner relationship as a model and a home setting

Many parents with young children are faced for the first time with demands and stress that means that some of their old ways of talking to their partner don't work so well. A basic rule in parenting is, 'Parents, look after your relationship with each other before you deal with the children.' A bad partner relationship means more stress and fewer resources to deal with the demands of children, and they get caught in the split dynamics.

The parent relationship sets the mood and comfort levels of the home. Most of the time, the home should be a haven of love and understanding in order to deal with an uncertain world outside the front door. It is also a model that the child will follow, whether the adults like it or not. We cannot ask children to delete the last ten minutes of their lives as they were not supposed to hear or see it. From now on those last ten, verbally abusive moments are part of the child's internal hard drive.

If parents have some stressful abusive relating going on, children will get the overflow just at a time when they need reassurance, not conflict. Reduced empathy for the other parent and more for oneself means that the parent has less empathy to give to children.

Children living with continual parental discord feel insecure and sad and ashamed of their home when with others, not to mention having divided loyalties and a desire to intervene, even in early childhood.

The following rules may help to avoid this:

- Make sure that your fights and unpleasant, 'over the top' and highly fragile moments are out of the sight and hearing of children. The very act of moving the conversation out of range will chill it anyway. Having said that, it is important for children to witness a model for conflict, so...

- Make sure that what children do see is a model of fair and respectful 'fighting' that demonstrates listening, assertion, empathy and conflict resolution.

The four-part phrase

A basic communication model

The following formula for communication is simple, powerful and effective, and takes just a little time and application. It has saved many relationships and made many more relationships happier than they were.

It is easy for professionals to teach communication, not only to parents but also to children. And it is suggested that professionals themselves consistently model the construct of the four-part phrase. Professionals should use both its 'positive' and 'assertive change' forms in the withdrawal room with parents. The following is addressed to parents so that it can be copied and handed to them.

I FEEL… [MY FEELING]

Using 'I' is important as it means you are talking about yourself and you should at least be an expert on that. Don't accept anyone telling you what you feel. You are the person inside your skin so you should know what you feel. Don't use 'you'. Whenever you do this people expect to be attacked or blamed and it immediately puts people on guard. Next, you also have to know *what* you are feeling. This may be difficult for some. Don't say what you think – use a feeling. First try vulnerable feelings like *fear, sadness, hurt and loneliness, left out, unimportant*. Then if you don't get the result that you want, try anger words like *upset, annoyed, angry*.

WHEN… [THE SITUATION]

'When' simply describes the situation in hand that created the feeling. Again try not to say 'you' but use 'it' or 'I'.

BECAUSE… [THE REASON]

'Because' gives the reason why I feel like I do when a thing happens. People usually respond well to being given a reason. If the reason is going to be argued with or questioned then don't give it. Your feeling should be enough.

I WOULD LIKE/WANT/PREFER... [THE SOLUTION]

This part is hard for some as it is about having a plan about what would put it right. It is essential for hope and for feeling as if things have been put right. It needs to be practical and possible. Don't apologize as you say it. It needs to sound clear and as if you expect change.

A four-part statement could sound like this:

Partner:
'I feel disappointed
when I am left waiting past our agreed time
because it seems that I don't matter and I don't know what is happening.
I would like you to be on time so I can feel respected and important.'

Parent:
'I feel so pleased
when you clean your room
because it's much easier to find things in a tidy room.
I'd love you to do it again.'

Child:
'I feel angry, Dad,
when Jamie takes my pens
because they're mine from my birthday.
I want you to get them back.'

Don't forget any of the four parts. Learn the four beginnings by heart so that you don't have to think about them and they will sound a lot more natural. This works and can be used for anyone, child or adult.

Professionals will note that children learn the 'four-part phrase' by rote easier than adults. Although it may seem counter to a more reflective practice, they should insist on a rigid copying of the model until it is thoroughly memorized. Parents and educators are the best model for the child, but independent training and framing of responses for children can allow three- to five-year-olds to integrate the four-part phrase structure into their responses.

Parents should be encouraged to put the four-part phrase on the wall at home and practise it until it feels familiar and the framework becomes a natural response that flows without thinking.

Sometimes, making a game of learning and reminding each other is useful for children and parents.

THE FOUR-PART PHRASE

I feel…[my feeling]

When…[the situation]

Because…[the reason]

I would like/prefer/want…[the solution]

There is a fifth part that can be added when the user is fluent in the four parts. It is best used by caregivers when holding boundaries, when there is no change in response to the four-part phrase. It involves consequences. Professionals should coach parents or caregivers to be cautious in consequence setting, however:

- It is best to have the other person's agreement for consequences so it becomes contractual.

- Only have consequences that you are sure that you can deliver because if you can't follow up you will lose credibility.

If this doesn't happen, then I will…or

If this does happen, then I will…[reward]

Essential points for helpers

- The four-part phrase structure contains the essential parts of any communication. Don't miss any out. Note that when people are really fluent they may put things in a different order. This is okay.

- Rote learning is good and okay! The four parts need to be learned by rote because they need to come immediately to mind from an unconscious level. They soon become integrated into an individual's language response rather than parroted.

- 'I' messages are powerful and teach self-responsibility. The four-part phrase also demands responsibility from others when they hear it.

- It takes skill not to use 'you' in the 'When…' part of the phrase. Instead say 'when [this…] happens' or 'when I experience…'

- Giving the reason (the second part) is really difficult for some. If it's too hard, leave it out.

- Help identify issues and good phrases for under-fives.

- Although the fourth part asks for a solution, we need to remember the lesson that two-year-olds learn so painfully: we don't always get what we ask for. That's life, as others have choices too! However, it is still important to ask for it. It declares us as a person and creates an initiative.

- It can be used by anyone: parent, early childhood education worker, child, support worker, counsellor, partner.

- It can be used for positive experiences or thanks as well as assertion. We encourage modelling of gratitude using this model.

(Adapted from Whitehouse and Pudney 2003)

Have cards in your pocket to remind you to say:

'I feel…, When…, Because…, and I would like…'

'I feel…, When…, Because…, and I would like…'

'I feel…, When…, Because…, and I would like…'

The repetition and strict format soon become cemented.

Setting boundaries

Imagine a glass of water, without the glass. It has no shape or form to manage it and simply spills and runs all over the place without direction. Children are like that. They need shaping and forming to find usefulness and identity. Many parents struggle with that shaping and need assistance and coaching.

Parents do the shaping and forming the moment the child is born, and the responsibility, therefore, is to shape and form in the best way possible, which may not be the way the parent was shaped as a child. For a while parents are the container that the child grows into and is held by. We need to guard against leaks in the container, otherwise they will lose something of the child.

Strong boundaries give children that moulding and shaping. Children who grow up without boundaries have a 'lostness' about them, they are often directionless, seem spilt all over the place, are always seeking, often don't fit in, are unstructured and often find it hard to fit into an ordered or disciplined environment. They may spend a lot of time wandering around rather than going somewhere and purposely using their abilities.

Setting boundaries can be a thankless task as the children who need shaping often resist it and push the limits or complain about the way others have a different container. It needs to be done in the confidence that it is for the long-term best rather than the short-term present. It is the job of all who are in the child's sphere to shape the child's path and set boundaries without leaks or holes, and it is the task of professionals to assist carers in doing this consistently.

There are a number of steps that can help in setting and maintaining good boundaries, as follows.

Drawing the line

This means deciding what the boundaries will be. Parents and carers need to ask the questions:

'What's the limit that you will accept?'

'What is the rule?'

'How do things work around here?'

'What is the custom of this house?'

'What's *okay* and what's *not okay*?'

Parents need to define the 'what's not okay' behaviour, and say what the desired behaviour is.

Most parenting that runs into difficulty has been confused on the rules or unclear about the way that the family, class or community does things:

- A child may see others doing things that are against the rules without consequence or attention and become confused.
- A child may see parents modelling a breaking of the rules and become confused.
- It the rules are changed often, then children become confused.
- If the rules are too complex and hard to understand, they become confused.

Confusion is like water spilling all over the place, threatening order and shape. Where order is unclear there will be insecurity, and this will likely be followed by anger. Clarity about the way things work and the systems that are particular to a place need to be attended to.

Tyler's mum and dad needed to go away because his mum was having issues with her mental wellbeing and 'needed a rest'. Tyler had never been to another home as there was no extended family, so when a family of the local church offered to care for him it was a shock and very scary for a five-year-old. No one explained simple things like what you could do with washing, when to get up, and that you had to say good morning to people when you first saw them each day. Tyler stayed in his bedroom to avoid 'mistakes' and was even too scared to go to the toilet and consequently had washing problems. Tyler needed every little assumed way of doing things explained with love. Needless to say, Tyler was both relieved and angry with his parents on their return.

Some rules will be 'big rules' like:

'We don't hit people here.'

'We always keep the gate locked to keep small children in.'

'We always look twice for cars before we cross the road.'

'We take our shoes off at the door.'

Some will be smaller like:

'We only use this much toothpaste.'

'We put our clothes away.'

'We don't suck through our teeth.'

Such rules, guides and set practices allow us to feel secure in the multiple choices of life. They allow a sense of control over our world that gives security and a sense that the system is proficient. For a child there are some things that need to be clear and held to for guidance.

We need to coach parents and carers in systems, such as early childhood centres and learning organisations, about how to deliver and hold such security.

First: *What are the rules?* We need to be really clear and to not have any disagreement or contrary opinions on regulation. Do all parents/teachers agree? Have you said what you *want* to happen as well as what you *don't want* to happen?

Second: *Are you serious about the rules?* Are all members of the team prepared to put energy into maintaining the rules? Half-heartedness will kill the rule as it will set up inconsistent delivery. If you are not serious, forget them.

Third: *Try to make the rules positive.* Describe the behaviour that you really want. Young children who hear just what they mustn't do will often remember it better than what they need to positively do.

Have some sort of reward, especially when they are new. Rewards can be slowly withdrawn as the rule becomes the practice.

Having decided about the practice and organisation you want, the rules need to be implemented. The following becomes important to holding order and security. These things are especially true for boys. Given that boys are often discussed with professionals as 'problems', the issue of giving and holding boundaries is worthy of professional enquiry and support.

Communicate the rules clearly

One of the easiest ways to create a hole in your boundary setting is to not have a clear agreement:

- Purposefully sit down and speak clearly and directly with the young child.
- Keep eye contact and be sure that they understand the seriousness and importance to you. The more meaning that you can put into the communication, the more impact it will have.
- *Give reasons why it is like that.* Check that those reasons are understood. Sometimes this is not possible so it may simply have to be a rule. If children are older, say four years plus, there is a growing ability to negotiate the rule so that it is something that you make up between you, but it must conform with other rules if there are others at the same age or stage.
- Say what you would really like to happen so the child knows the desired behaviour. Seek agreement and a sense of contract.
- *Check that everything is understood.* Ask the child to say back what they have heard.

What's the consequence?

- *Consequences are not punishment.* Punishment is based on revenge or payback. It is someone using power to pay someone back and is usually created after the event by the person doing the punishing.
- *Consequences are part of a deal or a contract* that people usually have some choice or negotiation in. They are known beforehand so that everyone has a choice and acts knowingly. You can even talk with preschoolers about what would be a fair consequence if they broke the rule. You may have to adjust their ideas of consequences. You need the same consequence for all.
- *Try to get the child's agreement to the consequence.* It always works best that way because it feels like a mutual contract. However, you are the adult with experience and have the power to make the final decision. The key thing is that the child knows beforehand what is going to happen.
- *Ask yourself if the consequence is reasonable.* Is it possible to carry out? It should be short and important to the child. Long consequences such as losing your

swing for four weeks do not work, as the child adapts after a few days. Losing the swing for one or two days would be far more effective.

- *Never threaten what you can't carry out.* If you fail to carry out the consequence, you will be taken less seriously.

- *Rewards: make sure you have plenty of positive consequences too.* Having plenty of rewards and reward systems is essential for preschoolers when you are coaching them in basic behaviours of life, such as toilet training, social behaviour, eating, relating to brothers and sisters, going to bed and personal functions. Notice them when they are good, and make good things happen as a result of their behaviour.

Celine is 22 months old. She delights in tipping out her toy basket and emptying her bookshelf. One day she began to put some toys back in the basket. 'Wow that's great!' said her dad. 'You are putting your toys away. Well done!' Celine looked up at the positive tone of Dad's voice and put more toys in the basket. Dad smiled. Celine put in more toys. Next day she looked across at Dad after she had emptied her toys out and began to put the toys away. When Dad said, 'Well done!' Celine put more toys in the basket. Gradually, with positive reinforcement like this, over time Celine could be relied on usually to put her toys away. Mum and Dad tried to remember to offer praise and thanks.

Be consistent

Be consistent, be consistent, and be consistent

Consistency gives security and safety. Children love order. They like to know where they stand. It is a big, confusing world otherwise. They may act as if they don't like it and they may push it to see if it is real. They need to know that those who are responsible for them are strong in order to feel relaxed and secure.

Don't give in because of your need to be liked, or wanting them to smile or be happy. Your 'consideration of special circumstances' may mean that you avoid conflict but you are setting up for more conflict later on. This is especially true of boys.

Children respect people who keep their word

If you fail to keep your word then you can't be trusted and that leaves the child feeling uneasy in an unpredictable world. It will take at least ten times of total consistency to win back that confidence.

The really confusing bit: needs are different from rules

As we help and shape children into normally accepted ways of doing things, parents and carers will also recognize that they are not yet developmentally like older children and adults. They can't reason things out as they don't have the development or the language to say what is going on. You can't discipline children for things that they don't understand or that they can't control – for example, toilet needs and fear at things that we see as safe. Their needs may be very immediate and related to different needs for company, food and eating, sleeping, wakefulness and toileting, to name the essentials.

We have to adapt to young children's changes. Their needs can't be articulated in the same way as older children. Children's cravings get worse when they are angry, hungry or tired. It makes sense to take care of this even though it may not be tea time.

We know that children who are *responded* to under 18 months old are less likely to be needy later as children and adults (Hendrix 1988; Karr-Morse and Wiley 1997; Maldonado-Durán 2002). We need to be able to give a high degree of personal contact in order for children to later separate successfully from us. These sorts of things need to be done on the child's terms, not ours.

This may sound confusing having just spoken of rules and consistency. The key is that rules are different and need to be set around the child's ability to comply with them and the needs of a normal young child at whatever age that they are at.

A SPECIAL NOTE ON BOYS AND BOUNDARIES

The following has been very helpful to the understanding of women educators, carers and parents. It is recommended that professionals attend to the carers' awareness of gender difference around boys and their need for clear regulation, especially as they appear to present about 90 per cent of behaviour problems and as they are not achieving as well as girls in Western education systems (Biddulph 2003; Gurian 2002).

Boys need very clear boundaries, more clear than girls

Boys' brains are wired differently to girls' and as a result are more compartmentalized, require linear order and are somewhat black and white in processing.

Boys like rules and simplicity of rules

Instructions and rules delivered by women tend to be wordy and multi-stepped, and for boys this can be confusing and hard to follow. Don't say too much. Be direct. Be very clear. Many boys don't follow instructions because there are too many words and they only hear the first sentence. Repeat instructions step by step *as they are achieved.*

Boys have a strong sense of fairness

They need to know that the rule will be the same for everyone all the time. If you change the consequence or let people off you will reduce your credibility and increase confusion. When boys don't have clarity and fairness they often seek to sort it out themselves; this means that they may challenge your authority.

Boys require more consistency than girls

Girls and mothers tend to take into consideration a greater number of factors and variables when making a decision and, as a result, have what seem to boys to be inconsistent decisions and consequences. Your word is your word, so with boys it is more important for you to appear to be keeping the rule than considering all the circumstances.

Boys want you to be the boss

They don't want to be treated like an equal or a friend. They want to know that you are holding the power so they don't have to. They feel safe and secure if they know that you are running a tight, fair, ordered ship. If you don't, then they feel like they have to, and so may seem to challenge you. For this reason men and fathers may seem to have better discipline with boys. They talk the same talk and think the same thoughts. This makes fathers important in boundary setting and maintenance. If necessary, involve the father or get reinforcement from the father if you think he is going to assist.

How to establish co-operation from the young child

The expression of anger is about responding to a state of powerlessness. If we can reduce the powerlessness of both the adult and child, then we are reducing the likelihood of either choosing aggressive behaviour or having an interaction that is likely to increase a powerless reaction from the other.

Winning the *co-operation* of the child rather than increasing control and enforced compliance will reduce anger.

Teaching, practising and coaching the parent or the caregiving professional in some of the following responses will assist in winning co-operation.

Distraction

Young children respond well to quick changes of focus and interest. Changes of focus have an element of oddness or surprise about them. It is easier to win co-operation than it is to control negative behaviour. Instead of trying to shout and dominate, the caregiver should lower her voice to a whisper or take the child outside for energy release: run and dance or splash in puddles with her boots on, or push the caregiver on a swing.

Voice security

If the child is in danger or something needs to happen right now, it helps to lower and deepen your voice, adopt a firm tone and make strong eye contact. Slow, deliberate speech has a security and impact associated with it.

Responding on the child's own level

Getting down to a child's level of eye contact and co-operation helps communication. Parents who consistently move to a child's level to talk, match their vocabulary and have responsive availability will increase their chances of being able to do the same with their child in adolescence.

Restoring energy and nurture

After a confrontation a small child will probably respond to something soothing such as a cup of hot chocolate and a story or a cuddle and a song. The food or drink restores blood sugar levels and the nurture restores a sense of safety.

Sending the message: they are okay, their behaviour is not okay

Children need to know that they are always loved. When a misdemeanour has taken place it is important to let the child know it is her behaviour that is disliked, not her personally: 'It is not okay to hit,' rather than 'You are a naughty girl.'

Make it a game

Tidying up toys can seem a daunting task for a small child, especially if she is reluctant to stop play. To help the child along, create 'tidy up games' such as, 'You put away the red toys and I will put away the blue ones', or 'I will tidy this corner, you tidy that corner', or, 'I'll race you, let's see who can be first.'

Organisation brings a sense of personal control and power

Knowing the place, procedure and requirements for a process or activity give the child a sense of control and security. It helps, if possible, to keep toys on shelves rather than in a toy box. This way, children learn that each toy has a place where they can put it back. It also helps to keep pieces of toys from going astray – it is easy to see if a piece of a jigsaw puzzle is missing. It also makes finding things less frustrating for children and helps busy parents maintain a more ordered environment. Knowing that this event happens after that event gives routine that makes the day predictable and sure.

Describe the behaviour that you want

If we are stating a boundary it helps to frame it in positive language. 'You can go as far as this line on the path', not 'Don't go out of the gate.' 'Walk along the side of the pool', not 'Don't run.'

Use humour

Humour can be used to distract a child who is fractious. Small children love *surprises*: the toy teddy that is made to pop up from behind the couch or the bubbles that appear from a bubble pipe and dance through the air. *Exaggeration* invites challenge and humour of the ridiculous. *Impossible statements* that are within a child's comprehension invite careful thought and advocacy of the child's perception over the adult, thus building critique and confidence – for example, 'crocodiles can fly'.

Music and movement soothes

Music can be used to soothe and distract a child: marching music or music in waltz time, or any music with a clear beat and rhythm. Dance with the child and teach her to dance on her own while performing other tasks.

Warnings allow more child control

It helps if we give a child warning of a change in activity: 'When the big hand on the clock is on the 5 we will be going to the shops'; 'Very soon it will be bed time'; 'When I have hung out the washing we will be going to the park'; 'You have only a little time to finish that.'

Stand in the child's shoes

Sometimes children hurt other children. This can be very upsetting for the other child and also for the parents of the 'offender'. Small children may have many reasons for doing this. Sometimes they are copying other people. Sometimes they are very angry or hurt. Putting ourselves into the child's shoes can help us to understand what the child needs. We can empathize openly with the fact that perhaps Mum has been giving a lot of attention to another child or adult, but it is important that we also let the child know that bad behaviour is not okay.

Replace with the positive instead of punishing the deficit

Punishment can be powerfully negative. If we assume that the negative behaviour was due to powerlessness or a painful situation, we can better understand how we can put something right and replace a deficit.

Helena and her small children belonged to a playgroup. One day a small boy began biting other children in the group. Helena was very embarrassed and was inclined to publicly punish him due to her public embarrassment. The other mothers talked about it and worked out some strategies to help. They made sure that the little boy got lots of positive attention. When he seemed about to bite, the nearest parent would step in and distract him. If a child was bitten, that child got lots of caring attention while the biter was given a firm message that biting is not okay and then ignored for a few minutes, while positive attention continued to be given to the other child. The biter was given lots of positive things to do with his anger such as stamping, jumping, screwing up newspaper and scribbling with crayons while his angry feelings were reflected back to him. 'It looks like you are very angry. It's okay to jump hard when you are angry. Show me how angry you are.'

Being hard on the behaviour and compassionate on the person allows for safety to be attended to as well as some creative responses.

Set limits for yourself

Parents need to be encouraged to set limits for themselves. They need time out to relax and often need their own space. They can teach children to respect their needs and help them to cope with parental self-care and for the child to play alone.

Show respect for child-space

This can be encouraged by knocking on the door of a play hut or tent before disturbing a child, or knocking on the door of their room before entering. The parent or care could announce, 'Excuse me, it will be time for tea soon.' It is also respectful of a child's need to gain completion of a project and to be in control of that completion. The acknowledgement of territory, both permanent and temporary, is useful: 'This is your little house and since you asked, I'll keep your brother away.' Modelling respect for others enables children to learn the same respect.

Show respect for their activities and creations

Completion is very important to boys. Space may be needed in a territorial manner in order to protect an activity: 'Would you like me to put it up on the shelf so that you can show it to your parents?'; 'Let's keep your construction safe by…' Regular warnings of a soon-to-happen change in activity can allow him to finish or stage his project or activity and enjoy some completion.

How to respond when a child gets it wrong

Contrary to popular belief, it is children who are severely punished who become anti-social members of society, not those who experience positive limit setting (Fergusson and Lynsky 1997). Children who are harshly punished feel helpless and hopeless, and may also begin to believe that they are inherently bad.

Zoe was struggling to set limits for her two small children. She was fluctuating between 'letting them get away with things' and 'being too tough'. Zoe recalled that her own parents were very tough on her.

'I could never get it right. I would be deprived of anything good for days, even for doing something small like not putting away my toys straight away. I don't want to be that harsh with my own children and when I do set limits for them I feel mean.'

Assist small children

Working with small children as a professional or as a parent is a unique situation. You must be constantly in empathy to the extent that you can deduct from clues sufficient conclusions to make up for the child's inability to self-analyse their feelings and to personally communicate them to you (as you would expect an adult to be able to do).

Additionally, we need to assist small children to make things right as much as possible. A small child can be shown how to clean up spilt liquids and other mess. If we show children that we understand how they might be feeling when they are distressed, they will then be able to empathize with others and in turn help others. Unless they are completely out of their depth, doing the correction for them completely may not be enabling but coaching in dependence and the use of others.

Model desirable behaviour

Children learn from what we do, not what we say. Action that is experienced provides a powerful imprint on the psyche.

When Jemma hurt herself her parents would cuddle her and soothe her and 'kiss it better'. When Jemma was 22 months old her father came home one day with a headache. Jemma climbed up onto the sofa beside him and kissed his forehead and said, 'All better Daddy.'

Apologize if you need to

Children need a model of behaviour for dealing with making a mistake. The lack of an ability to apologize suggests two things: the person is so well defended that they find it hard to engage in intimacy and vulnerability, and that they are always right, which is rather contradicted by the results and presents a dilemma of credibility.

Jemma's parents remembered to apologize to Jemma if they did something hurtful. Not long after her second birthday Jemma began to say 'sorry' if she did something hurtful.

Having parents who are unable to admit fault provides an example of modelling resolute invulnerability, which is good for fighting wars but useless for intimate, co-operative relationships. Older children also report it as a reason for feeling angry with their parents (Pudney and Whitehouse 2001).

> Put things right. Remember the four Rs:
>
> - Be **Responsible**.
> - Express **Regret**.
> - Make **Reparation**.
> - Experience **Redemption**.
>
> Cleaning up mess and mistakes leaves less residual anger in those affected. We need to help our children to make up for their mistakes if possible, and we need to help them to find ways to do this.

Responsibility

Children and adults need to accept responsibility if they have made a mistake or hurt someone else. Statements as clear as 'I did it' and 'I didn't meant to drop it on Kelly' indicate responsibility.

Regret

Regret or sorrow at the action require a degree of humility that involves the release of defences that are often used for appearances and a defence against shame and embarrassment. Children can be taught to be sorry for their mistakes by example. In this way their apologies will be sincere. We may need to point out to a small child that 'Mummy got hurt when you threw the block across the room. Did you mean to do that?' 'You made Grandma sad when you broke it' invites an expression of regret.

Reparation

Children, groups of people and adults need to have the belief that if one makes a mistake, then they need to fix it. That may mean a monetary cost for an adult, but for a child it is usually action and comment. Parents and caregivers facilitate reparation.

'What are you going to do about it?'

'How can we put this right again?'

'You broke Grandma's vase when you were running around inside. About that... What are you going to do?'

Reparation may be that the child comes and helps to clean up the mess, gives Grandma a hug and says, 'I am sorry.' Caregivers can also help children to not repeat their mistakes:

'How can you try to make sure you don't break something else?'

'I can play chase outside next time.'

Redemption

When we help children to redeem themselves we are helping them to function well in relationships and in the wider community. The acts of responsibility, regret and reparation automatically induce another to express forgiveness or to have empathy to the wrongdoer that allows empathic reconnection or inclusion back into a friendship or group again. The act is letting go of, and the relationship is redeemed. This process is used very effectively in the restorative justice process.

Where do they learn to behave like that?
Modelling and parental influence

We are continually learning from our environment and our experiences of our environment. When we are very young this is generally limited to just one or two people and, as we grow, it expands to many people. The most powerful learning experiences are those we experience in the first year as we 'install our basic software' that allows us to run the program of life. Mothers and fathers are therefore hugely influential.

There are other places young children learn from – brothers and sisters, friends, early childhood centres, nurseries, nursery nurses, television, looking out of the car window and so on, but the most important place by far is from the parent, both individually and from the environment that parents' interactions generate.

It is easy for any adult, when we don't like the behaviour or unhappiness or anger that we see in our child, to search around for reasons outside of ourselves, other influences, as to where they got it from. But children learn most things primarily from parents in the first three years (Irwin, Siddiqi and Hertzman 2007). These include language, how to relate to others, whether they are good and worthy of love and respect, and whether the world is a safe and happy place.

This is often hard for parents to accept when they are struggling with issues or with each other, and such a responsibility seems like another burden to carry. It is difficult when parents have been trying to do the best that they can. This should never, however, preclude them doing better with additional help, knowledge and coaching (we cover supporting parents in more detail in Chapter 9). The power of parents as a foundation influence is magnified by the huge dependence that babies and children have on them. Parents are the child's world, their safety and their security. If parents do something hurtful, it has a much greater effect on the child than if a stranger did it because parents are the home base and foundation of love, trust, comfort, security, self-esteem and safety. They are the origins of the blueprint of a child's life, the child's biggest model for life.

The length and intensity of time a child has with a parent is a powerful influence. Parents have usually known and influenced children for the entirety of their lives. The television, the car window, watching others at nursery, while they exist, can be turned off, ignored or walked away from; they have much less power or influence. When the parents interact, they are relating directly to the child as someone who cares about and matters to the child, so it is very real and has a much deeper effect.

Nearly all of this learning happens inside the child's home. Homes have a level of privacy and secrecy that may allow negative things to be hidden, although they never stay secret and unaccounted for. Accountability occurs as others experience children and report or support or question past parenting. Children in their teens also come to a point when they call their parents to account for the way they have been parented, and they may show anger or hurt that they have carried since early childhood.

It is too late when the child tells the parent at the age of 16 that she felt unhappy and afraid when the parent did something when she was four. The effect of the past is by then deep within the child, and it is also likely that the adolescent wouldn't tell the parent anyway, but just leave the parents wondering where they went wrong. If other people advise the parent that their child is a problem or has a problem, parents are likely to make it someone else's fault. Helping practitioners may find it useful to encourage parents by first asking them to consider:

'What could I be doing that could be causing that?'

'What significant things have happened for him/her in our house?'

'What behaviour am I modelling to my children?'

'What is causing hurt, fear, loss, insecurity in this home?'

This gives an effective, responsible and empowering base to work from because blaming sources outside of the home rarely leaves opportunity for immediate change or repair.

Resiliency

Building resiliency resources assists a child (and later, an adult) to have hope and to bounce with bad things rather than absorb them and crash. For children under five this is a prime time for building resiliency due to the power of the 'basic software' that the parents are writing for the young child's life (Bartley 2006; Irwin *et al.* 2007).

The following are important for nurturing and building resilience in children:

- building trusting relationships that don't frighten and which protect
- developing from that trust the ability for the child to ask for help
- framing life as a positive experience and the admiration and affirmation of an adult to assist the child to view from their strengths rather than despair
- assisting the child with change so that they gain a sense that change delivers other opportunities and excitement rather than insecurity

- building motivation towards short- and long-term goals, from 'Let's get those blocks in the box', through to, 'So you want to be a fireman?'

- taking notice of children so that they sense that they are important and worthy; listening to the feelings and dilemmas of the child

- modelling the taking of action and not procrastinating

- solving problems with the child and giving her a sense of agency, that there is *always* something that can be done about anything

- creating opportunity for excitement about the world and exploration; stimulating with things to be investigated

- using language that is positive and hopeful; admiring what is and aspiring to what isn't

- talking about things in context so that they stay in perspective – a late taxi doesn't mean that you have been abandoned or that Mum and Dad will lose their entire holiday

- believing that everything can be fixed or sorted out – there is a solution that will prevent this happening again

- giving self-care but also ensuring that the child learns by model and attention, that she is worthy of self-care and can do self-care for herself: 'I'm a bit cold, Dad. Can I have my coat?'

The cuddle factor

Dr John Briere poses the question of how a ten-year-old child who has suffered recent abuse is highly traumatized and devastated by the experience while another child the same age and gender is affected much less and bounces back to life much more easily (Briere 2003). He collects many of the elements spoken of above together in something he simply calls the 'cuddle factor'. This is where the caregiver or parent of a young child has extraordinary power to deliver most of the above by giving as much love, affection, cuddling, touching, positive encouragement, affirmation and safety as it is possible to give. The 'cuddle factor' is the parent's capacity to offer unconditional affection and love. It is not necessarily the parent's availability and empathy to offer conditions for the child's attachment, nor the parent's responsiveness to the child's efforts to attach. With the 'cuddle factor' the parent is likely to produce a child who can cope when bad things happen to her later, at whatever age: 9 or 49. It is the 'cuddle factor' that gives us that base belief that life is a good thing, I am worthy, and things will get better, as opposed to a feeling of devastation and worthlessness. High 'cuddle factors' in early parenting equip the child for launching into the rest of her life with a sense that she deserves to be here and that she can tackle anything.

Preventing provocative behaviour

Avoiding boredom: things to do with babies, toddlers and young children

Children often seek to generate attention by provocative behaviour when they are bored, which often generates angry responses from others that in turn are responded to from a 'fight' response. Parents and caregivers of young children need a repertoire of ideas for keeping active, enquiring, adventurous children amused and busy. Children are more likely to be interested for a longer time by items that require interaction, demanding their input into what the toy is and what it can be used for. Thus, playing with the wrapping paper after receiving a present may well be more interesting after a rubber doll inside has squawked a few times. And toys do not have to be expensive – boxes can become beds and houses in a manner that can hold attention for hours.

Here are a few ideas:

- Young children will use cardboard boxes for hours as they become boats, trains, huts or other constructs of a child's imagination.

- Ice cream containers can be made into posting boxes for babies and toddlers. Make the holes smaller and different shapes as the child gets older and more capable.

- Clothes pegs can be used for sorting into colours, types or sizes.

- Simple jigsaws can be made from packaging, magazine or greeting card pictures glued onto cardboard. Pictures can be cut, at first, with straight edges into three or four pieces. As children become more adept, pictures can be cut into more pieces and more complex shapes. Put the same symbol on the back of each piece of the puzzle so that they can easily be kept together. Store the pieces in envelopes. If possible, stick a photocopy of the picture on the envelope.

- Show small children where they can draw. Have a place where drawing paper is stored. Children will be happy to draw on off-cuts of wallpaper, the backs of greetings cards, wrapping paper and even newspaper.

- Small children like to paste things onto paper. Glue can be made from flour and water although it will only keep for a short while. Glue pens are cheap and easy for a child to use. Children will enjoy pasting pictures from magazines or greetings cards onto boxes and cartons. The box that held a new stove or other large household appliance will make a little playhouse and can be decorated with cut-out pictures. Small children will enjoy tearing out pictures. Older children can learn to use blunt-ended scissors. Smaller cardboard boxes can be glued together to make constructions and then painted or decorated with torn or cut-out pictures.

- Painted shapes and cut-out pictures can be hung from a wire coat hanger to make mobiles.

- Simple cooking helps children discover how ingredients change to make food. They can be given opportunities to taste and smell ingredients and feel textures. They can learn the words and enjoy the processes of grating, mixing, rolling and spreading. Jellies can be made and put to set in various shaped containers such as egg cups or yoghurt containers.

- Ice blocks flavoured with fruit juice can be made using ice trays or other containers. Children can help to poach or boil an egg and see how it changes in consistency.

- Children will enjoy being given pieces of pizza pastry to make their own pizzas with toppings of fruit, dried fruit, jam, cheese, spaghetti and whatever the child suggests (although you may not like it!).

- Water play is soothing and fun. Children will be happy with a washing-up bowl or a baby bath. Provide cups, cleaned-out plastic containers, a jug, a sieve, pieces of wood, plastic toys, a funnel. Stay with your child for safety, and by talking with her about her activities you can develop her vocabulary with new words such as float, sink, full, empty, wet, dry, cold, almost full, pour, tip, under, measure.

- Carpentry: to start with children will need a simple workbench. This could be made from a log of wood cut in half or a cut-down old table or coffee table. Children will need a light, adult-style hammer, flat head nails and some off-cuts of soft wood. You can help a child learn to hammer nails by showing how to start the process by holding the nail with fingers or a pair of pliers. You may hammer 20 nails in so that they can be finished off. Children can begin by hammering nails into a log. Later you might want to add a small saw and a vice, and perhaps a magnet to pick up spilt nails. Children will enjoy painting their constructions with water-based paints.

- Finger painting: to make the paint, in a saucepan mix ½ cup of cornflour with ½ cup of cold water. Add 1 cup of boiling water. Bring to the boil on the stove. Place 2 to 3 tablespoons in a small basin. Add 1 teaspoon of non-toxic powder paint and mix. Place a blob on a smooth surface such as a stainless steel bench or a metal tray. Two different colours will help children to discover what happens when two colours are mixed. Children can make patterns with a comb, sponge, nailbrush or a comb cut from cardboard. Prints can be made from a child's designs by pressing clean paper lightly onto the finger painting. Talk about how anger is a red colour. Play with red.

• Outside play: three- or four-year-olds will enjoy the adventure and fun of creating their own outdoor play environment. Parents can provide: small planks of wood, wooden or cardboard boxes, old tyres, sacking, old curtains or sheets, pieces of hose, a vacuum cleaner hose, logs, large sheets of corrugated cardboard. Parents may need to trigger a child's imagination by making something simple. Four-year-olds, who are increasingly able to play co-operatively with others, will enjoy working together and firing each other's imagination. Adults need to be able to watch small children from a distance to ensure safety. Watch interactions for co-operation and relational responsiveness.

• Sand play: little children will enjoy digging with their hands, sifting, patting and moulding. Older preschoolers will use their imagination to build and mould the sand into roads and hills and buildings. You will need clean, fine river or beach sand. You can make a frame to hold the sand with concrete

blocks or wood, or, if you are able to acquire a tractor tyre for a frame, children will have comfortable seating around the edge. Cover the sand when it is not in use so that cats and other animals do not get into it. Plastic netting attached to wood is ideal. Sand pit toys might include a spade, a plastic rake, buckets and containers, sieves and funnels, shells, small sticks, old cooking utensils. Watch for co-operative construction and ability to accept hierarchy of leadership. Children are not equal and boys especially are conscious of hierarchy. It is important that power and leadership are used and accepted respectfully.

• Pretend play: from about the age of two, children begin to pretend in their play. This is valuable to them. They can practise roles and skills they will need later in life. They act out what they see in their world and make sense of this. Pretend play also helps a child to express feelings. Help your child by providing old adult clothing, shoes and hats, a plastic tea set, old cooking utensils, cardboard boxes and cartons, old curtains, a cardboard crown, masks, a blanket that can be used as a tent or playhouse.

Exercise: Manual expression of anger with playdough

Playdough is a favourite with small children. Not only can it be used to encourage creativity, but it can also be used to thump and squeeze to express anger – a distressed child may find it soothing to punch and roll it. We suggest verbalizing while playing through sound and word and the adult sitting down, joining in and asking gentle questions to assist the process.

This is a recipe that can be made in larger amounts and stored for several weeks in the freezer:

1 cup of flour

½ cup of salt

2 teaspoons cream of tartar

2 tablespoons of oil

1 cup of water

A few drops of food colouring

Cook on a low heat, stirring all the time until the mixture is of playdough consistency.

Providing emotional language

Human communication is by words or body action or expression. Clearly, to varying degrees, a child under five has much less language than an older child or an adult. A child under two clearly has less language than a child over two, so there will be a greater reliance on body language and action, and this is a contributing factor to tantrum expression. The developmental task of a child under five is to shift communication from body action to words.

An angry child has both stress and a limited vocabulary to hinder expression when experiencing feeling anger. This is where some boundaries are needed. It is okay to wave one's hands about and bang the table with frustration but it is not okay to hit or scare people or break things. The building of an emotional vocabulary is vital, and adults who have not done this are at a disadvantage in relationships as feeling words are essential for intimacy.

The teaching of 'emotion words' is important. Many adults coming to anger management groups have fewer than three anger words, and these are often swear words. This affects their relationships and ability to get on with others. We need a large collection of words for all emotions so that we can communicate how we feel.

When a young child can't find the words to tell a parent or another child how she feels, the energy and frustration go to her hands, feet and face to communicate. This is okay for expression as long as no one gets hurt, but it doesn't necessarily help the parent know how to fix it and take the problem away. We need to teach our children at least ten words for each emotion so that they experience less frustration and we can know what they are feeling. Words give people exact meanings where sign language is still a guessing game. More anger vocabulary allows not just degrees of anger but also qualities of anger, such as the difference between frustration and vengefulness.

The main way we learn words is by hearing other people use them. Parents may be challenged about their own vocabularies and the way they may use them.

'Do you have big anger words like rage and furious?'

'Do you have small anger words like irritation and annoyed?'

Adults need the words for emotions – hurt, sadness, fear, happiness etc. Emotional literacy is now recognized as an essential tool for employment and business relationships, and many adults are having to find out what it means and start having an emotional life in order to relate to people in the workplace. Teaching a child now saves misunderstanding, now and in the future. It also allows a child to tell a parent or a therapist what is wrong, without acting out or engaging in mute guessing games.

Practitioners and parents may try using the following words daily as they relate to children:

angry, frustrated, cross, grumpy, resentful, jealous, vengeful, enraged, mad, bitter, wild, irate, livid, annoyed, cross, furious (see also p.47)

A good collection of anger words gives appropriate options instead of swearing.

There are also words that are not emotions that people use to convey anger. These may be body functions, exclamations and swearing. They all convey anger usefully but have less appropriate uses and can also mean several things. 'Upset', for example, can mean both sad and angry. The following are words that preschoolers may use to indicate anger. They are not enough for later communication, however, and need to be replaced:

'Don't, not fair, nah, no, I don't like you, go away.'

'You're not my friend, stop, hurts, don't look.'

'I hate you, shut up, I can't hear you, stop talking.'

Parents' use of words is the most effective way of learning them. The modelling gives context and approval. On hearing these words a parent may say something like, 'So you hate me *and feel angry with me*', or, 'So you feel like stamping *and you feel angry*.' This connects the feelings and the child's words and actions to the word *anger* and so she learns that this sensation is called anger.

Practitioners need to use more anger words and connect them with the child's feelings and actions. In many cases the work also includes equipping the parent with anger words.

Chapter 4

Identifying and Understanding Angry Behaviour

Levels of anger: body barometers

The tension/anger scale

Most people only become aware of their anger when it is at quite a high level. In order to manage it better we need to be aware of it at lower levels as well. This is harder and requires us to be more sensitive to our bodies. Adults need to know their very own individual signs of feeling angry and to talk about these with their children (check this out on pp.89–93). It is our experience from training situations that many professionals do not have a great awareness of varieties of anger and sensitivity at lower levels. We encourage them to consider their own relationship with, and awareness of, anger.

Another way of getting children and adults to be more conscious of levels of anger is to think of their body as an anger barometer, using their body to touch 'levels'.

Ask, 'How high is your anger? Is it a little anger, like up to your socks (touch ankles), or is it more up to your knees? That's being pretty annoyed. Or is it up to your tummy when you are really grumpy, or is it up to your chest when you are really angry and maybe up to your shoulders when you are really mad, but it could be up to your nose when you are really furious and you need to leave the room and calm down? Where is your anger up to?'

Children quickly get the idea and will tell you spontaneously. Basic numeracy can also be initiated by learning to count, starting at ankles as 1 on the scale and going through to the top of the head as 10.

Exercise: Working out the level of anger using the Anger Scale

1. Start with counting up the body to learn the degree of anger.
2. Develop different anger words to go with each level.
3. Name the body sensations that go with each level.

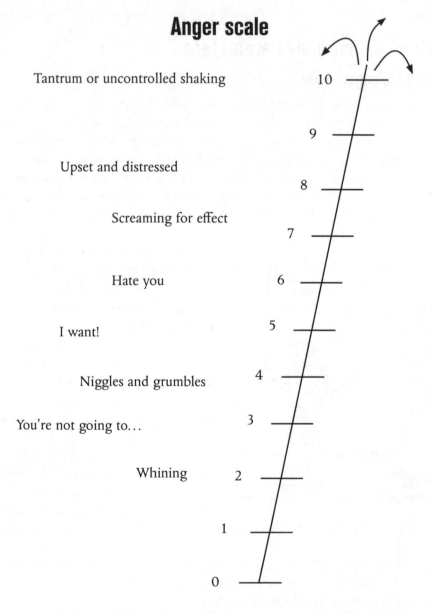

Anger scale

Tantrum or uncontrolled shaking — 10

9

Upset and distressed

8

Screaming for effect

7

Hate you — 6

I want! — 5

Niggles and grumbles — 4

You're not going to… — 3

Whining — 2

1

0

Source: Pudney and Whitehouse 2003

The Anger Scale is, perhaps the most commonly and widely used tool to assist with raising awareness of anger. The purpose of raising awareness is to give a greater amount of time to make decisions that are constructive and non-abusive. It also allows earlier attention to small angers and so prevents a stack-up of issues that are unexpressed.

Three types of anger

There are three types of anger that the Anger Scale can be used for. This is true for both adults and children. They are:

- immediate anger
- stacked anger
- deep anger.

Immediate (or single issue) anger

Immediate anger:

- is something that has happened recently, probably today
- is in our consciousness – we can be directly aware of it
- may often be about small things, like 'She tricked me'
- is identifiable as to the cause
- has an instant, charged response that soon dies down
- can be fixed fairly easily
- goes away.

It is the anger that we mostly associate with feeling angry in a day-to-day way. For the caregiver or child:

- Explain the barometer effect of the Anger Scale.
- Explain that blowing the top of the scale is not okay and results in the abuse of others.
- Explain that most people only notice anger when it is in the 7–10 range. This does not give much time to make good decisions. What we need to learn is to monitor anger at much lower levels.

Immediate anger should be easy for a caregiver or child to talk about. It may be as simple as, 'I am angry about having to give Grandma my room and having to sleep in Nick's room. She won't let me get my things.' Help the child talk about it and have a plan to put things right.

Stacked (or multiple issue) anger

This occurs when we have incidents throughout the day or week that pile up as unprocessed and together total a large amount of anger. Small incidents happen every day to everyone. When they are not resolved or acted upon they build up, and we use terms such as 'bottling up', 'having a bad day', 'stress build-up'. While one big thing might take us up the scale, many small things may also take us up the scale if they are not expressed or attended to.

It is possible to deal with each incident by answering these two questions:

- What action can I take so that I limit the possibility of it happening again?
- How can I release this and let go right now?

The Anger Scale allows us to track the small angers as well as the bigger angers and, through maintenance, keep the anger level at the bottom of the scale.

Exercise: Avoiding 'stacked anger'

Give examples of how we are going through the day 'winding up'.

1. Identify each small incident.

2. Think of an action that restores some power.

3. Consciously let go of the incident and return to 1 on the Anger Scale.

With small children good observation and detection is needed to do the above on their behalf. For example:

'You looked really angry when Jason took your book. Shall we ask Jason to give it back?'

'Let's take a deep breath and let that feeling go so we can feel happy again. Come and talk to me about some of the upset things that have happened today.'

Stacked anger is often saved and dumped on someone we love who doesn't deserve it. We do it knowing that, regardless, they will be friendly no matter how angry we feel. Parents may have stacking anger and come home and dump it on their children. Help them unpack the dump. Watch out for children who bring stacked anger from issues such as parents going off to work, not finding something that they want, or being made to do something that they don't want to do.

Deep anger issues

These may be carried around without us realizing that we are holding or carrying issues. We may not know about them and they may have been there for a while. An adult or a child could then be waking in the morning with a higher level of anger before even starting the day. This means less room to move in with the smaller ups and downs of the day. Small triggers may set us off for a big 'blow' that surprises us.

Deep anger usually has some of the following features:

- It is old or in the past.
- It may have been a bigger incident that has left wounds that have not gone away.
- It is often unconscious or semi-conscious – we don't know that it is there or we have forgotten about it.
- It hangs around and depresses us, nagging at our self-esteem and life force.
- It may shoot a charge out at unexpected times. The charge flows out through smaller angers and so makes the smaller anger seem bigger and out of proportion, and the anger may surprise us, and others, in its intensity.
- It hangs around until healed, let go of, or dealt with.
- It is not usually fixed easily and may need professional help.
- It is triggered by words, incidents, memories and familiar people, happenings or topics.
- It affects our sense of self-worth and personal dignity.
- It is caused by abuse, hurt, loss, domination, regret, shame or fear.
- It may be expressed by blaming and attacking or withdrawal.
- It is sometimes called 'dirty anger' or 'festering anger'.

The key to using the Anger Scale is to get it to become part of the child's or a class's conversation and a normal part of discussion. It becomes normal to ask, 'How high did you go?' with the response 'I shot up two points.' Everyone needs to talk the same language and to know what this means. Encourage checking anger levels at random during the day. It could be the start of a therapeutic discussion: 'How high did you go on the Anger Scale this week?'; 'Tell me what caused that'; 'How did you deal with that?'; 'What was a better way?'

Ideas for application

There are many versions or adaptations that can come from this exercise and creative alteration is encouraged:

- Colour in the anger/incident, use movable level markers, and speak the number level.
- Use basic maths; for example, sister teases = 2, accused of lying = 3, can't find my books = 1, my money has been stolen = 4. 'How high am I if all of these happen?'
- Have an object move up and down the wall as an indicator for a named person.
- Talk about a similar time when you handled this on the scale.
- Affirm methods of expression and good communication.

There are many adaptations for displaying the Anger Scale in a manner that suits the person/child. Some suggestions are:

- drawing a thermometer scale on a large piece of card on the wall
- using your body as a thermometer or container filling from the toes to the top (head); indicate this on your body
- putting a line scale on the fridge and using fridge magnets to indicate the different members of the family
- drawing it in a book and marking the date and time of your anger level at the moment of entry, or a maximum for that day
- using a graduated pole or stick to show your level
- using a large picture of a thermometer or a geyser or a ladder on the classroom wall and putting students' levels on it
- using the distance between your hands (stretching them out, or using fingers for short distances).

(Adapted from Pudney 2005, pp.18–19)

Deep anger is harder to track and it requires adults to do the tracking by looking at the big picture of the child's life and asking what bad things have happened to him. Think, 'When did these symptoms start? What seems to trigger them? When does he go quiet, and when does he get upset?' You may not like admitting or acknowledging some of those things because it feels as if you have failed to protect a child. Be as honest as you dare.

Exercise: Working out a plan: detecting and naming anger

Use the list of reasons for why children feel angry to ask specifically if a thing has happened.

Why small children may feel angry

- Put down in front of others at home.
- Left in the care of others for long periods.
- Not been noticed or paid attention to.
- Made to do things that they can't do.
- Called names by brothers, sisters or peers.
- Called names by parents or caregivers.
- Bullied at early childhood centres.
- Shamed in front of other children.
- Have seen others hurt around them.
- Have experienced crisis and trauma in the past.
- Not having the language to express what they want to say.
- Being forced to share.
- Having to eat food that they hate.
- Unable to do things that they don't have the skills to do yet.
- Being strapped or confined in one position for too long – for example, in a car seat or a cot with straps.
- Being hungry.
- Suffering sores or rashes.
- Being dropped.
- Being shaken.
- Have soiled their clothes.
- Being with strange people or in strange places.
- Not having both parents in their life.
- Having parents who fight.

- Being told to go away when they are trying to say something.
- Having parents tell them not to get angry.
- Having parents who are too busy to listen to their anger or hurts.
- Having had a younger brother or sister born.
- Being tricked, deceived or lied to by an adult.
- Being sexually, emotionally or physically abused.
- Being punished for showing anger.
- Watching a parent get hit.
- Being hurt by accident.
- Rigid or tight holding.
- Jealousy of other children.
- Wanting to go with someone when they are not allowed to.
- Made to do things, without explanation, that they didn't want to do.
- Having parents who split up.
- Not having things that other children have.
- Having a dad who rarely praises them.
- Having a parent who rarely says he or she loves them.
- Having a parent who drinks too much.
- Having a parent who has an addiction.
- Having a parent who doesn't have clear thoughts, is stressed or mentally struggling.
- Having a parent who hits or smacks.
- Having a parent who puts the other parent down.
- Having a parent who doesn't have enough time for them.
- Having a parent who is physically disabled.
- Having a parent who over-controls them.
- Being denied things.
- Unfair shares of something.
- Having an important person or pet die.
- Not getting something they really wanted.
- Being left out.
- Being shouted at.

- Having a parent who doesn't keep his or her word.
- Having to go to foster care.
- Feeling abandoned and alone and not sure that their caregiver will come back.
- Moving home or bedroom.
- Having angry parents or caregivers.
- Being left waiting for a parent for a long time.

An empathic exercise is to imagine a child's voice say: 'If you were willing to listen to me and I had the words of a bigger person, I might tell you that sometimes I feel angry because I have had an accident, I am jealous of other children, or I am upset about something at home.'

Parents should ask, 'Has this happened either in my care or with someone else?' Then, 'Has there been enough love and consistent care to heal the past?'

Tracking a child's anger

The 'Anger flow' diagram

Anger arises out of a sense of powerlessness based on our beliefs and expectations of what is fair, normal and just. To repeat earlier assertions, anger is a helpful emotional response to put right that powerlessness.

It is important that all professional helpers understand this in their own lives as well as the lives of the children whom they work with. Very often helpers have to work with an adult caregiver, other professionals and themselves in relation to a child so it is important that they can apply the principles of tracking anger to themselves as well as the child.

Referring to the 'Anger flow' diagram, the powerlessness mentioned above sits at the top.

'Anger flow' diagram

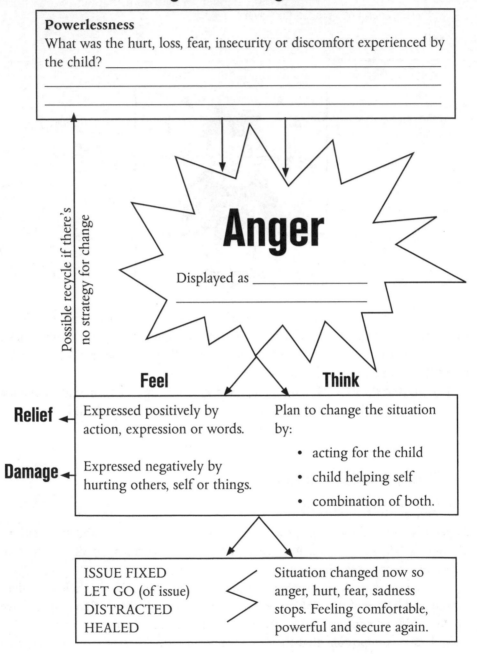

Powerlessness
What was the hurt, loss, fear, insecurity or discomfort experienced by the child? _____
_____
_____

Possible recycle if there's no strategy for change

Anger

Displayed as _____
_____

Feel   **Think**

Relief ← Expressed positively by action, expression or words.

Plan to change the situation by:

Damage ← Expressed negatively by hurting others, self or things.

- acting for the child
- child helping self
- combination of both.

ISSUE FIXED
LET GO (of issue)
DISTRACTED
HEALED

Situation changed now so anger, hurt, fear, sadness stops. Feeling comfortable, powerful and secure again.

1. The first task is to track back to the powerlessness behind the anger

The sense of powerlessness and insecurity behind anger comes from experiencing hurt or losing something or having something taken away from us or being denied something that we believe we are entitled to. We also experience powerlessness when we *fear* that those things could happen or will soon happen. Some hurts, losses, fears or discomforts are:

- *abuse*: loss of safety, security and trust
- *loss of possessions*: from a felt-tip pen to a bedroom
- *breakage*: loss of an item, and powerlessness to keep things whole
- *realization that the world doesn't exist just for you*: loss of self-importance and loss of control of others
- *rules*: loss of freedom and autonomy
- *parent left home*: loss of parent, security and love, abandonment
- *broken promise*: loss of trust and promised event
- *a death*: loss of a close person or animal, powerlessness over death
- *hunger*: feelings of discomfort or even threat of survival (for example, 'My tummy hurts')
- *being bossed around*: loss of personal choice, no autonomy.

There are, of course, many more reasons, both specific and general, why a child or an adult may feel angry. However, the loss of possession or attention, belongings or territory, the loss of a loved person (for example, a parent who has left the home), both physical and emotional pain, and the loss of rights or autonomy cover most incidents.

Young children have little awareness and fewer words to detect and communicate the powerlessness that they are experiencing. Professional helpers must watch, listen for clues and assist the child in gaining awareness through checking with them or simply supplying the need to see if it has solved the problem. This is quite different to working with older children and adults who need to develop personal responsibility for identifying the powerlessness themselves and communicating it. Professionals in early childhood must be wise detectives, often working on the child's behalf.

Having ascertained the powerlessness, follow the 'Anger flow' diagram to the next stage of the anger box. This will have been the thing that you noticed that led you to ask what was behind it. It is appropriate that you noticed this box first as the nature of anger is to call others' attention to oneself and the predicament.

It is normal to have noticeable anger over all of the above-mentioned causes of powerlessness and the many other events and interactions that are too various to mention. It is also good to identify how that feels for us personally as professionals and know that it is different for children due to their helplessness as young beings. Also note that anger has different causes in different children.

There are two things that the professional helper needs to do for the child's anger to remain healthy: to feel and to think.

Feel – we need to express that feeling (anger) in a way that doesn't hurt another person. Like walking, talking, making noise, doing something energetic, crying or shouting. Essentially this is done quite quickly and spontaneously in two ways: by body language or body action and by verbal or oral noise. Body action may vary from stamping, clenching a fist, banging or moving a hand, foot or instrument, running away, pushing a person away, refusing to do something, throwing, poking or shaking. All of these have a good and bad application – for example, poking the earth is okay but poking a baby is not; throwing paper on the floor is okay but throwing a stone at a window is not; letting out a roar is okay but calling a caregiver a bitch is not. One is okay expression and the other is abuse of another's rights, respect or happiness.

2. The question then is: how did the child express the anger?

Professional helpers have the wonderful opportunity of affecting behaviour and values before they become entrenched and habitual. It is far easier to teach social skills and norms to a three-year-old than a 33-year-old and even harder to a 53-year-old due to the entrenching of the neural pathways that make behaviour an automatic reaction rather than a choice.

It is vital that all opportunity to modify 'Not okay' behaviour under the age of five is taken and not ignored as, 'Oh he's just four and doesn't know what he is doing.' This is not true. He does know what he is doing, and if he didn't, it would still be the adult's task to let him know what he was doing and modify the behaviour with consequences. Many professionals endure spit, swearing, insults and kicks as 'he's upset' or 'he's having a hard time at home.' Impulse management starts at birth and particularly after two years, when the child has to take on that others have rights and that he is not the centre of the universe. Imagine the same child at 23, not three. The same kick given to you or another child is now many times harder and more dangerous. Its consequences involve doctors, hospitals and social services. It may also involve police courts, prisons, broken families and the next generation of a small child. Calling all 'Not okay' expression to account, showing healthy expression and holding clear consequences becomes a wonderful opportunity to assist that child to relate successfully to others.

The items in the 'Think' box in the 'Anger flow' diagram also need to be addressed. Many regard anger as an emotion that needs expressing, and that is it. This is only half of the story and half of the usefulness and purpose of anger. Moving from feeling to thinking mode is essential. Some people may even go to the thinking stage first and need to watch that they do the expression. Both are vital.

3. Has a plan been thought of to fix the problem of the powerlessness?

Think is the one that many people leave out. It means that you strategize or make a plan to put things right or to take away the powerlessness or hurt. If you fail to have a plan for yourself or a young child and act on that plan, then you risk the same thing happening again, maybe in ten minutes or in ten months. If you have too many repeats, the child ends up with a sense of hopelessness and becomes a victim, lacking in the knowledge that he is a powerful agent in his own environment. Having a sense of agency and ability to influence your environment powerfully is vital to the life that we are developing. Lack of legitimate agency and creation of effect in the world leads to illegitimate attempts to influence the world, and anti-social behaviour results. This same sense of agency must appear in professionals' work.

Many children have experienced powerlessness and insecurity so many times that they develop a way in the world that lacks confidence and is based on fear. The answer is to *act* and *to teach a child to act*. This may be as simple as: 'Come with me and I will hold your hand while you ask Sylvia to give your scissors back'; 'How can we fix this?'; 'What would you like to happen to make this better?'

Helping the child to act (to find and enact the solution), or acting on their behalf (responding to a distressed baby's cries and changing a nappy) lets a child know that he can do something about things that he encounters in life (Winnicott 1964). It also involves having a relationship interaction to change his situation. A child who has a sense of being able to do something about problems has a powerful attitude to step into life with. The child also doesn't have to continually feel angry in order to protect himself.

A child often feeling powerless and angry gets to be known as an angry person or a child who may generate a belief of not being loved and affirmed by the world. 'Victim' positions can be taken up and become clearly in evidence by adolescence, when they can become part of an identity. Anger is useful for getting yourself out of trouble. It gets attention. But it is no use if it is used to keep you in trouble.

The final question is a check-up: did the plan work, or is it likely to work in the future?

If the answer is 'No' then go back and do the third question again.

The key is to think, have a plan and then change things. After you have changed things you, or the child, should feel powerful and secure and happy again. Remember that it is not okay to feel powerful by controlling others' lives. It is not okay for a child to run a parent's life or for a parent to not pay attention to a young child's needs and security. In the end, other people and children get angry and hopeless. Professionals are involved in building an interaction based on the four questions and the diagram. Mostly, the incident can be worked through in a couple of minutes or, if it is a counselling session, it may become the basis for a one-hour reflection.

Sometimes, fixing a problem is not quite so solution-based. There are some things that require some acceptance, acknowledgement, processing/healing and letting go. What may need to happen is for an old wound or hurt to heal and for trust to be rebuilt. This is even more true of little children. A wound in the first few years has more influence than a wound in later years. Children who have been adopted, institutionalized, abused or a refugee in their first few years may spend the rest of their lives healing or compensating for this.

An example of letting go might be the successful processing of the death of a grandmother. There is no solution that involves bringing her back. The child, at her own level of cognitive development, goes through a process of coping, accepting and letting go. Support, care, listening, validation, empathy, reassurance, love and consideration all assist the process as part of the 'solution'. Healing processes take away the powerlessness, fear and damage, so long as action has been taken to prevent the same thing from happening again.

This model can be used for any angry adult or child.

Conner (two years old) feels angry. Going behind the anger we can guess that he is not just angry but hurt, and has had a major loss of attention because his sister has just been born. Not only does he feel the loss of attention but also at his age, he feels insecure with the change and the fact that he had to move his bedroom. People talk to him less and suddenly someone else has replaced him. He expresses it negatively by pinching his sister, kicking her bedroom door and losing some of his toilet training. This is not something parents need with the extra work of the new child and Dad having to do extra shifts. His parents could get very angry with him because they feel powerless and they could express it negatively by hitting him or locking him in his room.

They listen to his anger and because he is too small to say what it is all about they guess, with help from the local nurse, what the underlying problem is. They formulate a plan for him. They will purposefully spend more time with him, play with the baby and him together to develop a sense of sharing the joy. Dad will also take him on a special outing without the baby, a friend will give him a special baby gift, and for one night a week for a while he can sleep some of the night in his parents' bed. Conner responds because he feels important too now, and he feels included in the excitement about the baby. He has much less need to feel angry.

Referring back to the 'Anger flow' diagram on p.84, track back to the feelings of hurt, loss, shame or fear or the situation of powerlessness connected to the feelings. Ask what it is that could be causing the anger. Deal with that, rather than the anger.

Anger also needs to be expressed safely. Check if it was expressed safely by words, sounds or action. Then we need to know how we can change things, otherwise we could end up feeling powerless and angry again. What is the plan that would fix things or prevent you feeling like that again? Are you sure that it would stop the powerlessness happening again?

If we can't change things, we need to let go of whatever it is or go through a process of healing from the original hurt or loss. You should be left feeling calm and comfortable because the powerlessness has been taken away. The diagram can become a plan for dealing with every anger incident.

Warning signs of anger

Many claim that they have no warning of their anger and are unprepared to the extent that their anger has surprised and overwhelmed them. This is then used as a claim that they are not in control, and therefore not responsible.

It becomes serious if people are not in control, and the safety of the wider community must be considered if this is the case. Fortunately this is rarely the case. It just *seems* as if suddenly they 'saw red', 'lost it', 'went out of control', or 'went crazy'. If the helping practitioner can slow down the client's awareness so that small increments are detectable, it becomes clear that there were, in fact, moments of power assessment and a decision to do a particular behaviour.

Sometimes a parent can be challenged with, 'Do you think you would have lost it and struck out if a police officer had been watching?' The presence of such a superego figure adds sufficient weight to consciousness that it becomes unlikely that the parent would have lashed out. The task is both to transfer more of that superego regulator and also generate greater consciousness of a decision time that alternative, managed behaviour can take over. Developing a greater sensitivity of body awareness and small, early warning signs can assist in slowing down a whole incident and increasing choices of behaviour.

Children can be taught to increase awareness of their bodies and feelings more easily than adults. Helping practitioners, who have children in care for extended periods, such as care centres and nurseries, have the best chance of assisting awareness as they are on the spot when a real incident happens and can do awareness exercises in groups as part of their normal education function.

If we are aware of what happens to us when we feel angry, we have more time to make choices about what we are going to do. The better you know the warning signals, the better you will be able to deal with your anger. Early awareness can be divided into three areas:

- signs and sensations inside the body
- signs and behaviours outside the body
- thoughts and words that go on inside the head.

Imagine a recent situation where you were angry about something or angry with someone. See, hear and feel yourself there. Take yourself to the angriest moment, and then check out the early warning signs from the examples below. What are the signs that indicate you are feeling angry? Whenever you feel like this you can choose what you will do. You have extra time to do something positive.

Think of the child and a situation where he has expressed anger. What signs does he show of his anger? He will not know that these are his signs but you can help him by pointing out what they are by using the indicators below.

BODY SENSATIONS, SIGNS AND THOUGHTS

Mentally notice, check out and check off the following signs:

Two key questions are:

Do your cheeks feel hot?

What do you feel in your tummy?

BODY BEHAVIOUR (INSIDE)

Notice the feelings inside your body.

Heartbeat:	Fast	☐
Breathing:	Fast	☐
	Short	☐
	Deep	☐
Temperature:	Hot	☐
Head:	Bursting	☐
	Tense	☐
Jaw:	Tight	☐
	Rigid	☐
Gut:	Knotted	☐
	Exploding	☐
	Feel like crying	☐
	Churning	☐
Scalp:	Tingles	☐
Can hear and feel it		☐

Heavy in the chest	☐
Catch breath	☐
Sweating	☐
Red face	☐
Aching	☐
Teeth hurt	☐
Concrete lump	☐
Fire-like	☐
Hunger	☐
Hair prickles	☐

BODY BEHAVIOUR (OUTSIDE)

Notice the feelings outside your body and notice your body movements. These are things we often do if we're feeling angry.

Fold arms	☐
Agitated movement	☐
Tense toes	☐
Stand up	☐
Clench fists	☐
Clench jaw	☐
Staring eyes – squinting	☐
Walk away	☐
Frowning	☐
Tense laugh	☐
Purse lips	☐
'Evil eye'	☐
Stamp	☐
Tantrum	☐
Hit	☐
Squirm	☐
Hang head	☐
Pout	☐
Throw things	☐
Shout	☐

Twitch ☐

Tense eyes ☐

Not speak ☐

Say 'Nothing' ☐

Kick foot ☐

Narrow eyes ☐

'See red' ☐

Tears in eyes ☐

Bang walls ☐

Drink and eat ☐

Slam things down ☐

THOUGHTS

Notice the thoughts and sensations inside your body.

Can't think ☐

Withdraw inside self ☐

Pretend others aren't there ☐

'I'll kill my brother/sister!' ☐

'Go away' ☐

'You're not my friend!' ☐

'I'll hit you!' ☐

'You never help me' ☐

'I hate brothers/sisters!' ☐

'Stop talking!' ☐

'You wait!' ☐

'I hate you' ☐

Repeat 'mother' comments, 'You have to...' ☐

Fantasy of violence/revenge ☐

Scheming – 'I am going to...' ☐

'Leave me alone' ☐

'You can't play with me!' ☐

'I am running away!' ☐

'I'll get you' ☐

These are your unique signs and sensations. You will remember them.

Exercise: Recording body sensations

Draw a large shape of a body or ask the child to lie down and draw round the child's body shape. Write and draw a record of the sensations as the child remembers them. Recall them and talk about them. Use child language like 'I had caterpillars in my tummy,' 'My head went all on fire.' You can use the same language back to them when you are practising or watching and warning. Do some drawing of just colour of the different feelings as an incident progresses.

Introduce language like, 'I can feel like I am getting angry.' Do it as an adult. Many people find they start becoming aware of the smaller angers at the lower end of the Anger Scale as they become more sensitive. They start managing small angers.

Chapter 5

Calming Angry Children

Ideas for Safe Anger Expression

Time out and calming

Those with direct care for a child will be implementing these ideas first hand. For those who are assisting another with these techniques, it is important to take the parent or caregiver through the steps carefully and practise by role-play, to internalize the new responses.

Time out and calming for young children is different from time out for older children and adults. The main difference is the reduced ability to self-manage behaviour, depending on age, and the child's limited knowledge of the world and ability to understand what is happening around them and what solutions might be available.

A young child needs help to take time out until they are old enough to do it by themselves. This help involves:

- a caregiver noticing that the child is having trouble constructively managing behaviour

- a caregiver asking or suggesting that time out may be useful, or taking the child to time out because they are not able to talk sufficiently

- possibly going with the child to a time out place or mental state

- engaging in soothing or problem-solving talk

- helping solve the problem.

There are four ways that time out can be performed with young children, and choices about which to use will alter according to the child's age and situation. The following suggestions are ideas for home or for the nursery, playcentre, care centre, education centre or community child space. They are based on:

- distraction

- expression

- calming

- calming nurture.

Distraction

Young children have a very immediate focus of attention that can be easily shifted. The world can change almost immediately for very young children, and while they were raging and crying one moment, they can be interested and amused by something else within seconds. The shifting of focus by distraction can be done by the caregiver or parent, but the child may even do this herself. It is essential that the cause of the discomfort is attended (such as hunger, pain, soiled pants, possessions stolen or fear), otherwise there may be a return to the anger as soon as the distraction has lost the child's attention.

Words of distraction may be:

'Here, have this one.'

'Hey, look over here.'

'Come with me and we'll have a look at the fish.'

'I've got something special in my drawer.'

'Would you like me to tell you a story?'

'Isn't this pretty?'

'I'm thirsty. Want a drink with me?'

Acts of distraction may be:

- taking the child to different play
- drawing attention to something else
- doing a job with the child
- showing the child something special
- giving the child food and drink.

Expression

Children will naturally be more expressive than most adults. This is because they have not yet learned to repress their emotions, or because we simply expect children to be immediately honest and expressive. Expression is good. It gives an immediate release of emotions and is usually followed by a sense of satisfaction that allows the child to move on more quickly to something else. It would, in fact, be good for many adults to be more expressive, especially around anger. Repression, as the opposite to expression, is ultimately unhealthy except for giving sufficient time to carry it to a place where expression is appropriate. The spontaneity and passion that is needed for people to be happy is also very important in the work and relationships of adults.

The key to expression is to make sure that it doesn't hurt anyone, that it is genuine and that it lasts just for a limited time. For children, adults are the best trainers in expression as models of safe and healthy behaviour. At the early childhood stage this is mainly about non-verbal and kinaesthetic action (physically modelling action that children can copy).

Words of expression may be:

'Show me how it feels.'

'What do you want to do with your hands?'

'Make a face.'

'What sound does angry Stevie make?'

'It's okay to show me your anger.'

'Let's run.'

Acts of expression may be:

- having a go on the trampoline or swings
- drawing an angry picture
- moving to loud, fast, beating or energetic music
- ripping up paper (then cleaning it up) or screwing up paper (then cleaning it up)
- popping bubble paper with hands or an object or stamping on it
- running to the back fence
- having a go on a spacehopper (a bouncy toy)
- being a rocket blasting off
- performing a war dance
- whispering a swear word in an adult's ear
- using playdough or clay
- drumming
- safely hitting something soft with something soft
- hammering for a woodwork activity
- looking in a mirror and making faces
- digging a hole

- tearing Velcro apart (this could be specially made – for example, Velcro-covered table-tennis bats)
- stomping around in a pair of red wellington boots (a pair is available for children to put on and stomp about, when angry)
- pushing against a doorway or some fixed piece of equipment
- having a safe tantrum (see p.115)
- having a photograph taken of the child angry
- crying or laughing
- making a loud vocal noise outside
- talking to a different person about the anger
- playing monsters
- shouting at the wind.

Calming

Calming with small children first requires parents or caregivers to be calm themselves. Some parents need to do some practice with this as an essential skill in raising children and keeping them safe.

Children copy those close to them. If parents model 'calm', they are much more likely to 'hold' calm and stay there. If parents shout and act wild, the child will feel insecure and fear will smother any other emotion present. Here are some steps that should work, depending, of course, on the situation:

- Take some deep breaths.
- Count to ten.
- Lower your voice and slow it right down.
- Touch the child on the arm with a stroking or holding motion.
- Say the words that the child may not be able to say.
- Show the child an activity to keep the mind busy and attentive.
- Do that activity with them.

Many cultures have soothing games or activities (using a rosary or hand games). Using your body in small or gentle ways soothes stress. Some activities require thinking and concentration, such as juggling or building with blocks. This settles the child and allows problem-solving discussions. If appropriate, however, the child may just want the nurture of you holding her close.

Words of calming may be:

'Hey, steady there.'

'Slow down a minute and talk to me.'

'You are okay.'

'You're safe here.'

'Come close and talk to me.'

Acts of calming may be:

- playing with warm water
- playing with a worry doll
- guiding them to a thinking activity
- juggling things
- sitting down somewhere together
- going to the 'Thinking Chair' (Time Out Chair)
- singing
- counting to ten
- taking some deep breaths
- playing relaxing music
- going to the 'angry place' (a positive pre-set place)
- moving to a thinking activity such as building
- going outdoors and coming back in
- handling worry beads
- using the expression dolls (a doll with changeable expressions on its face)
- going to a pre-arranged time out place
- playing in the play hut
- going to the favourite tree (sitting under or climbing and sitting in the branches)
- holding a 'thinking ball' (a rubber Koosh ball).

Calming nurture

Calming nurture is really an extension of ordinary nurture. It has overt love and touch added. For professional helpers, some of this may be outside professional expectation. The touch and love must be safe for the child, otherwise trust will not be built and it may even be destroyed. If the action creates fear or surprise, then less intimate ways of nurture must be used. For example, for millennia water has been used for soothing and changing moods, attitudes and states. And animals have a remarkable ability to reassure, calm and heal children through the unconditional love that they give. Telling animals or dolls about any problems has been a wonderful lifesaver for many children.

Such calming is more about touching and healing the hurt than managing anger, and really is the essential and final stage in the 'making well' after anger.

Words of calming nurture:

- 'There, there, there…' (rhythmic talking)
- humming
- 'Daddy loves you.'
- 'You are such a great kid.'
- 'Stroke the cat and tell her your story.'
- 'Let's rub/wash all the hurt away.'
- singing.

Acts of calming nurture:

- stroking something soft like fur
- kissing it better
- cuddling, stroking an animal
- talking to an animal
- the adult having a cry as well
- giving the child a cuddle
- washing the child's face
- wiping/washing the cut or hurt place
- putting on bandages or plaster
- rubbing the child's back
- giving the child a bath
- holding something warm
- holding a cuddle rug
- wrapping in a 'blankie'
- stroking the child's hair.

Points to remember about time out for young children

- Time out helps to manage emotion and keep people safe.

- Time out doesn't fix the initial problem.

- Young children forget easily what the problem was. Adults have a responsibility to find out what the hurt or loss was, and go back and fix things so they don't happen again.

- Time out is a time to calm, soothe, relax or express and think.

- Sometime, either in time out or later, there needs to be a time for healing.

- Time out should be talked about beforehand, in a purposeful way.

- The child should choose a time out place.

- There should be a practice time out at first.

- Time out should not be a punishment – ever! The punishment place should be called another name. That way, it is not a bad place and children are happy to go there of their own accord later.

- Time out should be age-appropriate for the length of time and place. It should be for a set amount of time at first. Perhaps one minute for each year of the child's age.

- The parent or caregiver should go with the child to time out. The parent or caregiver starts with deciding when the child comes out and it then progresses to having the child deciding when to come out.

- Parents or caregivers may need to take the time out, not the child. They should do it and model it.

- Responsibility should be encouraged as early as possible. The child should be invited to go there or asked if they need to go there.

- Young children should always be kept visible.

- A frustrated parent may be afraid that they may hurt the child. The child should be put in a safe place and a friend called. At that point the parent needs the time out. They should not re-engage until they know that they are calm.

- Be consistent. Be consistent. Be consistent.

Time out for preschool centres

The basic principles are:

- Time out should be a time of safety, expression and calming.
- Time out should be a time for the parent or caregiver and the child to think about how to improve the situation.
- Time out should be non-destructive of self, others or things.
- The child or parent/caregiver should always be responsible for what they do.
- Time out is best with company for young children.
- Tracing the cause of the child's anger – for example, hurt, loss, fear or insecurity – should be carried out where this is possible.
- Things that are wrong should be put right.
- All abuse should have consequences.

Steps the parent/caregiver or child can take

- The child needs to know any boundaries that have been given around taking time out.
- The child needs time out clearly explained.
- The child can have an arrangement sign such as a gesture, statement or word that can be easily shown to indicate that the caregiver or the child needs time out.
- The child should be trained to take time out when she is fearful of losing control of herself or needs to calm down.
- The child should go to a time out place with no disruption.
- The caregiver must notice the child is in time out mode and must protect the child in that mode.
- The caregiver should affirm the decision to take time out and use soothing tones.
- The child should stay there for either an agreed amount of time, as long as the child wants or as long as she is accompanied by a caregiver.
- The child should then go back to the communal setting and either she or the caregiver should perform any task required to improve the situation.

- The caregiver should assist the child in tracking the initial cause of powerlessness, hurt, loss or fear of hurt and loss.
- The caregiver may assist the child to strategize for change, or may say what she is going to do to put things right.

Taking time in the 'Time Out Chair'

(This section is adapted from Whitehouse and Pudney 2003.)

Time out allows us to give ourselves time and space to think about safe ways of resolving problems. It also gives us an opportunity to see the other person's perspective. Time out is not a form of punishment. If we use it as a punishment, then children are not likely to use it proactively and so will miss out on a valuable way of managing anger – good anger management resolves a problem and doesn't just put an 'unpleasant emotion' out of sight.

Exercise: An idea for effective time out

1. When a child is calm and receptive, tell her the story of the 'Time Out Chair'. 'We are going to have a special chair in the house/centre. It will be called the "Time Out Chair".' Name the chair. 'It's going to be the... We are all going to use this chair to sit on when we feel really angry and we are worried we might break the Anger Rules.

   'Make sure that you sit on the chair when you are angry. Say out loud what you are doing. "I am furious. I am going to sit on the Time Out Chair." Express your angry feelings – for example, deep angry breathing. Follow this with slower calmer breathing. Talk about any ideas you have for resolving your problem – for example, "I shall clean out the cupboard at the weekend and then I will be able to find things more easily." Finish by saying, "I don't feel so angry now. I feel safe to get up now."'

2. Continue to do this as the need arises. Children learn best by observing others. Professionals need to continually ask whether it is the child or the parent who needs the Time Out Chair (or another anger management tool).

3. Next time the child seems out of control, direct her to the Time Out Chair. Small children may not go. You may need to take the child to the chair and hold her on your lap. Do not give positive reinforcement until the child calms down. Then tell her she can go and play now, and that you are pleased with her.

4. Remember the principle that children have to learn safe limits to their behaviour. If they can't yet do this for themselves, adults must provide safe limits for them.

5. The Time Out Chair should be portable. It can be a chair at Grandma's, a seat in the park, a chair in the waiting room, or even a time out square or bench on the floor in the supermarket.

6. This only works if parents/caregivers continue to model it and reinforce the behaviour with praise and recognition. Again the model needs to be genuine.

7. We all need to practise safe time out behaviour.

Helping a small child cope with strong feelings

- Stay with the child.

- A distressed child may want to be held, but an angry child may not.

- If possible, make eye contact with the child and mirror the child's feelings in your facial expression and eyes.

- Get down to a child's level so that the child feels that you are with her.

- Say something that lets a child know that you understand. 'You feel sad when you can't go and play with Annie?' Use a slightly questioning tone so that the child has the chance to correct you.

- If a child is throwing a tantrum, leave space between you for this to happen, but stay within sight. Don't give attention to the tantrum; stay as neutral as possible but remain present. A small child can be quite frightened of the power of her own anger. Be ready to talk afterwards and hold the child – it is not possible to reason with a child who is throwing a tantrum. Attempts to reason may cause more fury if they are seen as attempts to control. If the child is in danger of hurting herself at this time you may need to hold her firmly. Sometimes a tantrum can be stopped early with distraction.

Gemma was throwing a tantrum because she did not want to get into her car seat when she was out with Grandad. Grandad quickly said, 'Hey there's a dog just like Hairy Maclary' (book character). Gemma immediately stopped screaming and looked around to find the dog and forgot about her anger about being put in her car seat.

Daniel would throw tantrums in the late afternoon but his caregiver soon realized that these could be avoided if a small snack was provided. The caregiver forgot that the energy and tolerance of a small child is less than ours when out shopping or visiting. It is not hard to come across a distressed child being dragged around the shops, towed along by an angry, frustrated parent. It is likely that the child is well past the time to go home.

The caregiver was warned that Sophie was prone to tantrums.

The caregiver found this was true but, by reading early indicators, surrounded her with soft reassuring words, attention and comfort without 'smothering' when she showed signs of distress and strong emotions, such as anger sadness, grief and despair.

Learning to self-soothe and contain herself as a child is a good skill for adulthood. This prevented Sophie from getting overwhelmed by her own emotions.

Children prone to distress build-up

Exercise: Using a sharing scrapbook

Get a scrapbook with plain pages and a packet of crayons for each child and give ten minutes to each child each day.

The purpose of the sharing scrapbook is to:

- encourage good communication
- show a child that you are willing to listen
- develop self-esteem (we all feel more worthwhile if someone gives us their time)
- teach children the vocabulary of feelings – sad, excited, angry, disappointed, proud etc.

In an early years setting, the children should be told that they are going to have a ten-minute scrapbook sharing time every day. If another child in the family, centre or class interrupts, the time should be made up. If the interrupting child is aged three and up they will have some idea of sharing and time, and will need to pay it back from their ten minutes.

Find a quiet time and place to 'chat-and-scrap' about the day. Bed time or 'quiet time' is good if those occasions are available. The exercise is calming, and for a parent, by staggering bed times it can be possible to give each child in the family a turn. Also establish a regular routine such as: pack up toys, supper/snack, shower, pyjamas, sharing, storybook, bed time. In a centre it may include types of activity and food. Routine is reassuring, and the sense of order suggests that all is in control and the child knows what comes next and can expect it without becoming anxious. It helps a child get into a rhythm that is calming and leaves a child more willing to co-operate and share.

Method: Open the book to a double page. Ask the child to draw a picture on one page about something important that happened that day. On the other page write the story of what happened and, most importantly, how they felt when that happened – for example, 'Tom felt angry when Sue grabbed his lunch,' or 'Sue felt excited when Mrs Smith said they were going to the zoo.' As time goes on, the book becomes a favourite storybook and also a reference book. 'I remember another time when you were angry. Let's go back through the book and see.' Save these scrapbooks for later conversations and memories.

Chapter 6

Responding Well to Expressed Anger

The following is a short summary of how best to deal with a child who is in the midst of expressing his anger.

Exercise: Dealing with an angry child

- *Listen, appreciate, understand, soothe and validate.* Children need you to understand why they are angry, as if you were inside their skin having the same experience. This is the most important thing of all. Much of our anger disappears when we find that we are not alone and that we are understood by someone else who cares and listens carefully.

- *Track back to the hurt or loss.* Find the cause. Behind all anger there is a hurt or loss or fear that hurt will happen. Professionals, parents and/or caregivers need to work back behind the anger to find this. Babies need adults to do all the work because they can't tell you. Preschoolers can help with things that have just happened. Most children have trouble talking about the deep angers that happened some time ago. Sometimes it is guess work. The child should be helped to see the real cause behind the anger.

- *Develop a strategy for change.* Attempt to fix the cause of the problem. Talking about it makes us feel better but it doesn't fix the problem. If things don't change and the problem doesn't get fixed, then it may happen again. This is even more disempowering. Develop a strategy with the child, or support the older child's strategy if this is possible. Or you may have to fix it by yourself for a young child. Make sure that the child's world is as safe again as it can be.

- *Set boundaries.* If the child is abusive or undisciplined, or a danger to himself and others, set boundaries and consequences. Explain why and try to get the child's agreement. Set boundaries that are clear and understood by facing the child and engaging in serious communication. Ask, if the child is old enough, what would be a suitable consequence if the rule was broken. Set consequences that are realistic and clearly understood and, if possible, have agreement. Make a deal/contract. Check that you have co-operation. Be consistent about maintaining your boundaries and keeping your word. If you fail to keep your word then you are unreliable and untrustworthy. This leaves the child insecure. *Consistency* is the key to happy, secure and ordered parenting.

Responding more generally to a young child's anger

Young children are so limited in their language, their emotional recognition, experience of the world and possible solutions that adults have to do most of the work.

- Watch the child and look for signs of anger, hurt and loss when they occur.
- Listen to the clues that the child gives us in language.
- Feel it as if we are the child.
- Go behind the anger and find the hurt, loss and fear.
- Let the child know that we can understand some of how he feels and that we can understand what is going on.
- Give words to what it is and so voice what it is for the child.
- Check that we have got somewhere near the right understanding.
- Help the child find a solution.
- Help the child to put the solution into effect so that the problem is fixed.

Drawing pictures

Drawing pictures is a good way of starting when children can't talk about difficult things. This method is used by teachers, nurses, therapists and social workers for assisting children to open up and talk, indirectly at first, about difficult issues such as abuse, or issues where there is loyalty to parents and the family. Direct language and names can be left out to facilitate easy opening up.

Getting children to talk is one thing. It is even more difficult for them when they don't know what to say or they find it too hard to tell you what is going on. One way of assisting talking about things is to ask the child to draw a picture of his anger or the problem. This makes talking easier because:

- it is not inside him but on the paper
- he doesn't have to name things that are hard to name or unknown – he can just point to them on the paper
- you can do it again and again for the same problem and track progress
- you can also draw the solution.

You will need:

- paper and pastels, crayons, paint, chalk or very thick felt-tip pens; don't use pencils, fine felt-tip pens, ballpoint pens or sharp drawing tools
- respect for the child's way of telling the story
- to listen hard, as if you were the child
- to build trust and not be frustrated if you don't 'get it'
- a safe and quiet place where others can't overhear
- to not interpret or impose your own meaning
- to be thankful for the child sharing.

Invite the child to draw his anger or the problem or the thing that bothers him or something that he is unhappy with. (You may do this as a sharing scrapbook exercise, see pp.104–105.)

Sound interested and involved without suggesting things. Anything that gets drawn on the paper is just fine and is valid expression.

There are four ways that children and adults can express themselves with pictures:

- life-like representation
- symbols and shapes that mean something or represent real or imagined things
- moving their arms and fingers to express the feelings just by enjoying the physical action; this might look like scribble but it is the action that matters
- writing real or pretend words on the paper.

To facilitate the drawing, parents or caregivers or professional helpers may want to use the following phrases:

'Tell me the story about this.'

This could be followed with some of these other words if they seem appropriate:

'I bet there's a special story for this picture.'

'If there was a special story for this picture, what would it be?'

'I'm guessing this was a special time that you were angry.'

'What's happening in the story?'

'When was the last time that you were angry like that?'

'This bit's really interesting. Tell me about it.'

'I'm interested in...'

'I notice... Can you tell me about...?'

While you are chatting, look for:

- patterns
- central features
- lots of colour or black
- lines or boxes of containment.

Black may indicate depression, sometimes deep or stale anger. Red may indicate raw anger that is easily accessible. Green or yellow may indicate new things. Be very careful about interpreting the use of colour, however, as sometimes they are just favourite colours, the only colour available, colours done to please you or they may mean something else altogether. The meaning that the child gives to the colour, shape, density, action or picture is what matters. Do not pressure the child for reasons, meanings or names. He will tell you when he is ready, which may or may not be the next time – we talk when we are sure that we will not get hurt again or when we feel trust.

When he has finished talking and telling the story, ask:

'What do you think would fix this?'

'How could we make this better?'

'How would you like me to help?'

'What will you do now?/What would you like to do now?'

'If we could do magic, what would you make happen?'

You could conclude by seeing if the child wants to stop, seeing if he wants to draw the thing that fixes it, draw another picture altogether or come back to it a week later. Ask the child what he wants to do with the drawing. If it contains material that could embarrass the child, is confidential or just not very good, he may want to hide it, rip it up, put it in the bin or leave it in your safe keeping. It is not recommended that the child is public with it, such as hanging it on the wall.

Thank the child for sharing and assure him of safety, support, hope and solution.

In summary, the three steps are:

Step 1. Draw the picture

Step 2. Tell the story

Step 3. Discuss a strategy for change

Parents or caregivers who are puzzled or worried by the story that they hear should talk to professionals with specialist knowledge of children. Community nurses, counsellors, child therapists and social workers are used to hearing children talk and interpreting language, and may be good people to have a telephone discussion with.

Fights between children

Fights between children are common and are often seen as scenes of anger and hurt, especially between peers. They are, to some extent, a part of everyday life where people know each other well enough to say what they think and be themselves. It is an occasion to be real and uninhibited.

Children learn from fights or scraps. They learn how far they can push people, about their moods, about fairness, about consideration, about empathy for others, about not being afraid of anger and about how to stick up for themselves. Home is the safest place to practise this because they feel secure enough to know that they will still be loved and accepted afterwards. Childcare and learning centres are places where others are available to test individuality and rights, and to learn about the will of others. That may not seem so great, however, when parents or professional helpers have a headache, are stressed or are just exhausted after a long day.

Scraps between children also have a good level of spontaneous freedom in them. This is an opportunity to learn management of feelings and behaviour when being that free. Children also need to learn that adults have limits and tolerances that change as well. Adults sometimes need to intervene. For example, if it always seems to be Jess squealing at something that Zach did, then the parent is probably being set up with a 'rescue me' game. Children know about the rescue value of being a victim. Professional helpers and carers have an additional fear of parents complaining, and may get caught in that protector role out of fear of parental disapproval.

Many boys later in life express considerable anger at the way their younger sister or the baby of the family set them up by claiming to have been teased, bullied or treated unfairly. The unfairness is actually that the boy is left resentful and feeling devalued at the one-sided protection that he feels is going on, and this affects the younger person's power to make and act out untrue situations and dynamics. Interactions between older and younger, and boys and girls, often mean that a parent who dislikes the whine or the cry comes steaming into the lounge angry at the conflict and ends up laying blame or consequence on the boy or the older child. Fathers are particularly open to the 'con' as they imagine a challenge from the older male.

Perceived fairness is important in dealing with children's scraps and interpersonal anger. Parents who often have to intervene or rescue need to examine the situation for a 'set up' and consider laying responsibility on all the children involved.

ADVICE FOR PARENTS OF FIGHTING CHILDREN

Shut the door and act as if it's not happening. If one child yells out even louder to get attention and entice you to intervene, suggest saying, 'Settle it yourselves', then grit your teeth to manage all the old reactions that are bursting out of you. After about four to eight times the children will stop doing it because they aren't getting the result. You don't have to come to the rescue. The victim will soon learn that if you aren't there, it is not smart to trigger or annoy someone who is bigger. This is a life skill that they are gaining. There are other ways of handling people to get what you want. If it is an issue of an older child initiating the bullying, then professional helpers should do one or both of the following:

- Address the bullying behaviour separately from the interaction though talk, discussion and away from who is being bullied (they may then deliberately taunt the 'bully' as payback).

- Ask why the bully may be engaging in that behaviour and respond therapeutically. The most common causes are: bullying models, emotional deprivation, abuse or envy. (See also the section on attachment issues, Chapter 1.)

ADVICE FOR PROFESSIONAL HELPERS OF FIGHTING CHILDREN

The problem is more complex in institutions because the reports that parents receive from their children are very centred on their child's perception and because the likelihood of a bully in the centre is greater. If a child is showing that he cannot deal with a situation, then professionals are compelled to intervene for the emotional and physical wellbeing of both children involved. Again it is important for the professional to see both sides, and not just step in and 'rescue'. Failure to observe this will likely lead to entrenching victim and bully roles rather than resolving the incident. The preferred approach is to deal with both children separately or assist the awareness of both perspectives. Conflict rarely has just one psychopathic perpetrator. It is a learning opportunity between two wills.

Assist both children to try not to react, and to see another perspective: 'Marcus thinks that's his pen. Please ask before you use it.' 'Daniel doesn't like getting hit. We don't do that here. What would be a good way...' Or take both children aside separately and begin with boundary setting, then move to compassionate understanding and coaching for problem solving.

The rule is, don't get involved in responding to the immediate stimulus of a protest. Deal with the issues in a dual or separate context of reciprocal transaction between the two involved.

A SUGGESTION FOR RESOLVING PEER CONFLICT AT HOME

Put each child at opposite ends of the sofa, and tell them that they cannot move. Do not have the television on. They must stay there until they have sorted out their disagreement. Soon they will call you in and say, 'Can we go now?' You will ask 'Have you sorted it out?' They will sound uncertain and you will say, 'No you can't go until you have sorted it out!' The next time they call you they will probably have an agreement.

They soon realize that settling it gets rid of the boredom of being fixed to the spot. Be consistent about standards of conflict resolution. Some people put both parties outside and say they can't come in until they have settled the dispute – nothing less. It must be settled. Children need to learn the skills of dispute resolution instead of how to manipulate Dad or Mum as rescuers.

It is rare that anyone gets hurt in childhood scraps, but have strong rules and consequences about not allowing physical harm in your house.

Tantrums

A common concern of parents with young children is tantrums. Helping professionals are often asked for advice. Much of this concern comes from the:

- seemingly out-of-control nature of the event
- distress that many children experience
- appearance of poor parenting (parental embarrassment)
- risk of damage to the environment around the child
- idea that the child will be damaged.

Coaching parents or caregivers usually fairly quickly results in good management. The major issue is usually the caregiver's own personal fear of embarrassment or disaster. Tantrums generally are fine! It is some of our responses that are not.

Why do children throw tantrums?

Children throw tantrums for many reasons. Primarily they are a deep, physical expression of rage, which comes from a sense of powerlessness.

The young child has limited language – children need to express anger but do not have the language to do it. There are essentially two means of a person expressing anger:

- verbally/orally through words and sounds – swearing and shouting and pleading and complaining, but also oral noises such as roars, sighs and exclamations
- kinaesthetically through bodies, arms, legs and body language.

Obviously the young child is not just limited in language but specifically in emotional language, which is even harder to acquire due to its non-concrete nature. Tantrums then are a natural resort for the body to express extreme anger and frustration.

It is a developmental stage of childhood to have, over a period of time, the painful realization that you are not the centre of the universe and that there are other forces at work, such as others' choices and needs and demands that have to be reconciled with your own desire. This egocentric transition takes place usually in two- and three-year-olds. Thus there are extra reasons for feeling angry as a two-year-old.

There are other reasons that may lower a child's threshold to the survival emotion of anger:

- Children tend to throw tantrums when they are tired – ensure that they are getting enough sleep.
- Children tend to throw tantrums when they are hungry. When our blood sugar level is low we are all more likely to resort to anger to help us survive. Give children food and drink while you are listening to them. Ensure that your centre has adequate snack and meal breaks. Small bodies contain less fuel and are more active than adult bodies.
- Jealousy is a worthy reason and an additional burden of a damaged ego. This is likely to occur when attention has been drawn away by problems or other peers, when disappointed by the level or frequency of attention, when new babies arrive and 'steal the world away' and additionally add the insult of parents not only loving the new baby instead of the child, but demanding that the child loves it too, when the child feels like killing the baby (Winnicott 1971, 1980).

Tantrums and parents

Differentiating between power plays and distress, the three main reasons for tantrums are:

- healthy expression of anger
- power plays between parent and child
- distress and devastation for the child.

Healthy expression of anger

There are times when tantrums are a genuine expression of anger that needs to be done loudly or physically. That is the real purpose of a healthy tantrum – to vent frustration and to discharge anger. Most of us would do well to throw a tantrum now and again to get rid of stress and anger that has built up. Therapists, particularly, can become so repressed that a good tantrum at home or under supervision is recommended. Try one. It's quite invigorating! Even a pretend one works well.

There are two rules with tantrums:

- No one gets hurt and nothing gets broken.
- No one watches (except when the child is distressed and then nurture may be needed).

Observing these two rules makes the tantrum safe and takes away the performance aspect. It soon sorts out the genuine expression. Most genuine charges of anger don't last more than a minute; after that it becomes about performing. (See also pp.81–83 for help in finding the causes of a child's anger, pp.104–105 for the sharing scrapbook, and pp.107–110 for 'Drawing pictures'.)

THE TANTRUM RESPONSE RULES

- Leave the child alone.
- No one gets hurt.
- Nothing gets broken.
- Nobody watches.

Power plays between parent and child

Tantrums often hook the parent into:

- fixing things just as the tantrum thrower wants them fixed in order to get what they want
- feeling shamed or embarrassed in front of friends or in public – for the child this may not initially be intended, but he can learn that tantrums give him the power to shame the parent.

Distress and devastation for the child

Tantrums from a deep hurt are different. Deep distress tantrums, as opposed to performance tantrums, need soothing. This can usually be detected by a high level of deep sobbing from the child. In these circumstances the parent needs to bring the child back down from the distressed state as it is coming from fear and devastation. Soothing, calmness and love are needed.

More sensitively: what to do?

- Just listen and accept the feeling of rage from the child. There is a *good* reason for feeling it. Try to find out why the child is angry *before* the tantrum or if not, *after* the tantrum.

- Try finding a distraction when the tantrum is starting. Sound really surprised and interested in something else. Ask questions that require rational answers like 'Where?'; 'How many?' (for older children); 'Who?'; 'I want to help you with that.'

- If the child has a tantrum just sit it out and watch if they are very young and you may choose to be nearby instead if they are older. Stay very calm.

- If you said 'No' to something, don't change your mind just to gain the peace. Sweets and treats reward tantrums and teach the child that he can manipulate you. This is an important lesson for life that we all need to learn – that we can't always have our own way. This is an appropriate developmental age to learn it. When you say 'No' and mean it, it can also give the message that you are a good parent acting for the child's long-term good. You are maintaining a solid shape to their boundaries.

- There is a type of tantrum that is more about *desperate despair* and is likely in younger children. It is typified by a sense of desperation that can be picked up empathically and may be expressed by gasping, body-shaking and severe distress. A good response to this is soothing language and, at the right time, physical nurture/touching/stroking/holding. It will usually reduce to deep sobbing.

Shopping tantrums

This may be embarrassing for parents and they may report that the supermarket or shopping mall is the only place that this happens. Older children can sense this embarrassment and may find that tantrums are more easily rewarded in shops. First, it is important to always stay calm. Shopping trips should be kept short. Parents or caregivers must never hit the child – hitting often embarrasses many observers too and even makes some angry. A parent may decide to remove the child from the shop and to go outside to walk or to go to the car. Parents should not be afraid to ask for help from someone to carry the shopping bags if the child has to be carried.

Tantrums around the house or in the homes of others

- Parents may have strong reactions. The parent should never hit, bite or kick their child or verbally abuse him even though the parent has had the child do that to them. Doing the same act (payback) teaches the child to *do* those things, *not* to not do them.

- Parents should be encouraged to use role-play to give reasons why the child's behaviour is not okay, and to keep it simple: 'No, we do not bang plates because they break'; 'No, don't touch the power point. You could get hurt.'

- If there are other observers to the tantrum then they should be asked to leave.

- Professional helpers should suggest that the parent give love, thoughtfulness and regulation, *not* what the child is demanding from the parent.

- When the tantrum has stopped, the parent may give the child the time and attention they need. A few minutes' love and noticing can save a lot of time in the long run.

- Angry children may need a run in the park or some physical activity to express energy that may otherwise turn into a tantrum.

Tantrum ages

At two to three years old

Tantrums are common at around two to three years of age. Two-year-olds want some independence but this can be scary as well as exciting for the child. At this time parents or caregivers also need to keep the child safe. A balance needs to be kept between keeping the child safe and not squashing his moves towards autonomy. The fury being expressed is usually about the fact that the whole world isn't revolving around 'me'. This is a rude discovery for a child who has had a loving, caring home up to now, with parents who have been very protective and not wanted to see a baby/toddler in distress. It may be a shock for a parent too. This is the age when the child learns the power of saying 'NO' and individual defiance. The defiance is about the child's self-focus and entitlement to power in the world. There is an important development at stake here, however, and the child needs to learn that the universe isn't just there to satisfy his ego. The reality of having to wait, not getting what we want and having to think of others is one that faces us all and needs to be learned as a child.

At four years old

There may also be more tantrums in the fourth year as the child finds new ability, power and energy and new expectations of behaviour. Four-year-olds are more likely to be angry because their *adventurous behaviour* is being curtailed. Four-year olds are developing their initiative. They need to be kept safe but not have their development stifled.

Four-year-olds can be shown safe ways of expressing their anger, such as punching a pillow or their bed, hitting a tree or pole with a stick, jumping, stamping, drawing, scribbling on newspaper or talking about how they are feeling. Four-year-olds will also have greater ability 'to talk it out'. It may take time for some children to use these methods, but it is worth persevering.

Physical restraining

Physical restraining works best for the child who is distressed, upset, who may attack another and who needs safety and calming. It does not work well with power-play tantrums. It should never be used as a form of violence or straight domination.

It is an act of loving contact that allows the child to be safe and feel secure enough to reduce to the tears behind the anger. If it is just a fight with no love or tears, then physical restraining is not recommended. There is a growing paranoia of touching a child, however, but if we are to hold children's wellbeing at heart, we have to be willing to show embracing touch, physical rescue and genuine comfort, and this is especially so for boys, who have strong kinaesthetic needs. As kinaesthetic learners, expressers and experiencers of the world, both developing relationships and education can be hampered without this.

Physical restraining is the holding of a child in a way that restricts the child's arm and leg movements while he regains calm and emotional control. Many parents are afraid of such touching because it seems close to fighting. Done well it has no real chance of becoming a fight at all, however, and has a real quality of intimacy about it. It is *not a physical battle* but a loving embrace that a child will absorb and give in to. It is recommended for young children, and especially for boys.

The holding technique is done when there is a lack of control by the child and genuine distress. It is best done from behind, with adult arms securely holding the child's arms to their chest. It is best done on a chair or sofa that allows the adult to sit behind and not have to deal with kicking feet.

USING THE HOLDING TECHNIQUE

Keep your head to one side so that you don't get head-butted in the nose or chin and hold very securely. The idea is that you are supplying the control that the child doesn't have. He senses the containment and security of strong arms around him that is more reminiscent of a hug, and within that security is able to rely on you to protect him and manage him. Talk to him in a low, calming voice as you hold him secure so that he knows that this is a strong hold of nurture. Allow the rage to subside and usually it will go to tears, which is really what it is all about. You are then accessing the hurt and sadness that lies behind the anger. (See the diagram on tracking anger on p.84.) Hold him more loosely then and talk gently and reassuringly. He needs to sense love in the hold as well as strength. When he is calm let him turn around and have a cuddle or cradled embrace.

As this practice has been improperly implemented in the past, many care centres do not allow it. Professionals should check to see what the official policy of their organisation is before trying therapeutic holding. There may also be particular ways in which it is practised and also reporting procedures.

After a tantrum

Often children need soothing and comforting after a tantrum. A child will often be frightened by the force of his own anger. Body contact should be warm and reassuring and should not generate fear but security. Adults need to be discerning about whether a child is distraught and fearful or whether he is engaged in a power display. A trusted adult can give calm reassurance and can teach safety and provide a model of soothing. Adults need to be astute as to what is right for each child.

Dealing with bad language

Verbal expression can be a form of expressing anger. In itself it is essential to life and to be encouraged. All cultures have more expressive forms of verbal expression that tell people of the intensity of feeling they have.

Swearing falls into two forms:

- allowing fierce expression
- saying strong or forbidden words to show you are tough or dangerous or that you are devaluing others.

Only the first, allowing fierce expression, is condoned by us. For small children there is a sense of innocence that many parents would wish to preserve, even though they do the first kind of swearing themselves. 'Bad' words then are seen to be inappropriate for small children. Children often pick up swear words and enjoy their dangerousness. They may also use this language because it has been learned at home, or in their wider environment. If others in the environment use these words we are more likely to use the words too, because of a human need to belong.

Beth and Ian did not like swearing and did not swear themselves so they were surprised when Jemma began using two swear words. They felt very uneasy. Beth noticed that when they were out in the shopping mall or just walking down the street many people used these words and she began to see how Jemma had discovered them. Ian noticed that the words were on the films he watched on television. They were both upset at Jemma's bad language but did not know what to do because the more they reprimanded Jemma for this, the more she did it.

Parents and caregivers need to be very aware of their own language. Often, organisations and parents forbid the use of swear words by children and yet use these words themselves.

What to do if children use bad language

Toddlers and two-year-olds will probably be just 'parroting' what they have heard somewhere else. They won't know what the words mean. If too much fuss is made they will say the words more. It is best to ignore it as much as possible and praise the good things children say instead. Children of three or more may be using the word for conscious effect, however.

How to say very bad words

Childcare centres and early childhood education often have problems with creative responses to 'bad' words and swearing.

- A useful approach is to work either as a group or individually to make up a very expressive word that feels good to say. This obviously will not be a standard swear word or offensive in any way, but will sound as if it could be if you heard it in another language. Have an agreement that it *is* a 'bad' word then allow the use of the word as a special word when the child or carer feels angry.

- A child who insists on the use of a standard swear or profanity word may partially regulate himself by having an agreement that it is only okay if he comes up to the teacher or parent and whispers it in the teacher's ear. Generally the anger is well past by the time they get to you and even then it is confined to one person and the professional is in a perfect position to begin a conversation about 'What happened to make you feel that angry?'

POSSIBLE 'HIJACKED' EXPRESSIVE WORDS	IMAGINARY SWEAR WORDS
Hippopotamus	Frogalot
Pumpkins	Babolukes
Fishcakes	Shmishymash
Crabapples	Ragripper
Jacksnakes	Figrats
	Poppleslosh

Swearing is also an opportunity for young children to learn that there are different standards/codes/rules in different places. It is an important life lesson that there are some places where you can swear and others where you can't.

Respecting the right of a child to express their anger

Young children have a wonderful, untouched joy for life. This needs to be protected and directed. To curb, kill or crush this joy of spontaneity and exploration is a form of oppression, be it through deliberate negation or neglectful omission. Children who have had this damage and oppression have a right to be angry and may carry that anger for a long time.

Being able to foster the joy and spirit of life requires that a parent or caregiver has dealt with negative and life-restricting things that have happened to them. It is so easy to suffer from envy of the spontaneity and freedom of children and to act restrictively.

Adults at a family wedding reception watched with delight as a three-year-old child danced to the music. The little girl was full of the joys of life as she chatted to family and friends. She showed delight in others, no fear or shame, and people smiled infectiously when they saw her interacting with others and playing. Her parents received compliments for the joy that she expressed and drew out of others.

Unfortunately for some children this confidence and enthusiasm for life may be squashed out of them by the attitudes and limitations of adults in their lives. Most will know of someone who has difficulty motivating themselves, who seems unable to persevere and finish tasks, who has a sadness, who needs lots of approval, and who seems to be a 'crushed' person. There are many things that can 'crush' a child:

- neglect
- over-regulation
- physical, mental or sexual abuse
- a reliance on punishment as a way of disciplining a child
- lack of encouragement to be creative and to try out new things
- experiencing trauma, including family violence
- having an alcoholic or drug-taking parent
- lack of encouragement to learn.

In order to foster and develop that life-loving potential, children need encouragement, praise, love, interest, security and a hearty response to their feelings in order to enhance their life force.

Using reflection to reduce impulse behaviour

We live in an increasingly hyperactive world where there is pressure to zip, zap and buzz, to achieve more in a day. Reflective practices such as meditation, 'dreaming' or sitting in silence have been reduced to time snatched – for example, when sitting on public transport. Even jogging, usually a reflective time, is now often accompanied by earphones. Children need to witness models of contemplation and reflection as a base for both stress reduction and thought about self, actions and events that need attention and consideration. This reduced reflection time has contributed to impulse behaviour and reduced learning from experience. Pausing to reflect as adults, parents or caregivers allows us moments when we can stop, contemplate and review action, and also to step back and observe ourselves and ask questions about our quality of life. Reflection requires slowing, calming, coming into the present and self-observation. It is an opportunity, by expanding awareness, to increase compassion for self and others. A moment of stillness opens up a bigger picture that allows a spiritual sense of the world and relativity in the overall setting of a life.

Such reflection can be assisted by walks, meditation, stress stones and beads, chatting besides fires, staring at clouds and stars, eating together, writing, diaries and lying awake and listening to one's own breath.

The Buddhist teacher Thich Nhat Hanh (1987) suggested that the practice of mindfulness reduced the relentless passage of the day, allowing us to get off the train and to stop to appreciate the world and how we were really experiencing it. The stopping, calming, noticing ourselves and expressing gratitude allows a richness of life that could otherwise be missed. This is important for professionals, parents and carers as such moments of calm awareness reduce stress, anger and reaction, and increase learning. If we are calm and aware and responding with appreciation, then we have a better chance of responding to children well and also modelling peacefulness to the world. The connection between oneself and the child can become closer as we recognize that our state of mind is related to the child's state of mind.

Exercise: A mindfulness exercise for adults working with children

- Stop. Be here right now in this present moment.
- Concentrate on your breath. In and out. Nothing else is more important than your breath.
- You are watching everything from calmness and you are here right now, in the present.
- You watch yourself and the situation without judgement.
- Continue to watch each breath as different from the last.
- Your calmness and stillness allow kindness.

Children need to learn to stop and reflect. Young children should be taught to relax and to be still, to appreciate silence, to chat about the day, to think about what went wrong, to think of ways of putting things right, to feel secure with others, to talk about the things that are troubling, to ask about the bigger picture and philosophical things in a way that fits with the age of the child.

Exercise: Assisting children to be less reactive in their lives

In a group setting:

- Lie back and watch the clouds and look for shapes.
- Talk about thoughts or pictures or colours or words that come to mind.
- Ask about the day's/yesterday's happenings.
- Ask 'what if', 'why', 'how did' questions.
- Ask about what is worrying them.
- Lie in the grass.
- Watch water – rivers, drips, waterfalls, ponds, puddles.
- Watch birds.
- Touch things in nature.
- Ring a bell and ask everyone to 'freeze' for ten seconds.
- Watch candles burn.
- Ask, 'What are you thinking about?'
- Walk in silence.

Parents and/or caregivers can encourage the following at home:

- Talk at bed time with the lights off.
- Sit silently together.
- Invite the child to ask questions.
- Turn off the television and listen to all the small noises that appear.
- Listen to each other breathe.
- Discuss invisible things.
- Daydream.
- Talk to animals.
- Make long soft noises of the same note.
- Sit beside a real fire.
- Listen to birds.
- Introduce a child to 'the outdoors'.
- Look at pictures in books.

Chapter 7

Special Situations that Provoke Anger

Young children's ages and stages mean that there are particular situations, such as being left, grief and loss, and separating parents, where there are responses particular to their age. Some of these are covered here.

Anger and loss

Anger is part of the grief process and is expressed in different ways depending on the age, stage and understanding of the child. From the moment of birth we begin to experience loss. This may be as primal as loss of the comfort of a womb through to the loss of a nipple supplying food, the loss of the close mother relationship when we are weaned from the breast, the

loss of our familiar cot when we are moved into a bed, the loss of familiar favourite toys, the loss of unconditional, loving acceptance when we become mobile and need to be limited in our exploration. When there is change we experience loss. For some children there are more severe losses to be encountered, such as when parents separate or when a family member or pet dies.

Professionals may come to be aware of this loss by either the parents or through the child. Professional helpers may have to advocate for a child where parental losses are sufficiently intense for it to be hard for the parents to be there for the children who are also upset and grieving. Parents may not see, or even know, that their children are also grieving. If the parents are preoccupied with their own feelings, it is important that someone else takes responsibility for assisting the children, and so a professional helper may arrange for another to do this or be in some role of 'getting a child through' the upset in place of a distracted parent.

Death may be confusing. Small children do not understand the permanence of death and panic at the despair of adults and older children who are able to appreciate its finality.

Three-year-old Simon had a pet hen called Borky Bork. One day the hen died. Simon was distraught but the family helped him cope by having a funeral and burying Borky Bork in the garden. Mum read Simon the story called *The Tenth Good Thing About Barney* at bed time. Simon felt sad for a few days and asked for lots of hugs, but after a few days it seemed that he had forgotten about his pet. Then several weeks later in the spring Dad went out to dig the vegetable garden. Simon came running outside, 'Are you digging up Borky Bork, Daddy? Is she all better?' he asked.

Children progressively form an idea of permanence. They find it too hard to believe or imagine that they or a loved one could just disappear, although this is what they dread at some level, and this is the reason for their distress when left for a short while. This situation has much to do with attachment and the immediacy of love and security.

As children get older and try to make sense of the world around them, they will have many questions and fears regarding death, such as:

- Why did she die?
- What will happen to him now that he is dead?
- Where will she go?
- Will I see him again?
- If Grandma dies does that mean that Mum or Dad could die?
- Perhaps I could die too?

We need to be able to answer a child's questions simply and honestly from our own belief system, and should not give long, complicated answers; just answer what has been asked. It is important that we give answers that do not set up further fears for a child.

Danny's grandad had died. His mother told Danny that Grandad had 'gone for a big sleep.' For a long time Danny was afraid to go to sleep and when he did drop off to sleep he would wake in the night screaming. It was several nights before Mum realized that Danny believed that by going to sleep he would die too and that dying was bad.

Laurie was told that her uncle had died because he was sick. Laurie became very distressed any time someone in the family developed a cold, believing that they would die too.

If someone dies because of an illness, it is important that we tell a child that that person was *very, very* sick, and that having a cold or a tummy bug is just being a *little bit* sick. Sometimes, if appropriate, a visit to the dying person may let the child see just how sick the person is.

Often when a child or adult is afraid, they will cover their fear with anger. It is also a normal part of grieving to be angry about a loss or deprivation of something or someone we love. We may even be angry that the person has left us. 'How dare they die and leave me at a time like this?' If we don't allow ourselves to be angry and to talk about our anger, we can be stuck at the angry stage of grief, sometimes for years. Children, too, need to be helped through their anger at a loss.

Children need to be involved in the mourning of a loved one. There was a time when children were excluded from family funerals because it was believed that they would not understand. Adults sometimes present to counsellors as still coming to terms with a loss after many years because they were not included in the grieving process as a child.

'My brother died when I was four,' says Moira. 'One day he was there and we were playing together and the next day he disappeared. I was told he was not coming back and people around me were crying. On the day of his funeral I was sent to a neighbour's house. I felt so lost and alone. I did not understand what was happening. I am still angry that my parents did that to me.'

Children need to be listened to and to have their questions answered. They need to feel that adults understand how they are feeling. Adults need to be available to answer their questions over and over again until they reach a stage of accepting that the loved one has gone and won't be back. Even then, just like adults, they will go through periods of extreme sadness and anger when they are reminded poignantly of their loss.

Isabel was five when her granny died. Her parents took her to the funeral and answered her many questions. Every time they passed the cemetery she would say, 'That's where Granny is.' At night, for many weeks, Isabel would ask the same questions: 'Are you and Daddy going to die? Will I die? Why did Granny die?' Her parents would give the same answers every night and afterwards Isabel would turn over and go to sleep.

Mum and Dad made a photo album of photos of Granny that Isabel could look at and talk about. Gradually she only needed to ask the questions occasionally and then the questions stopped.

Often, when a family is experiencing a loss, the parents are so involved with their own grief that it is hard for them to be available for their children. At such times other family members or friends need to be there for the children. And children need to be told why their parents are so distracted. This is the point at which the third parent or extended family may reduce a child's trauma and give security.

Professional helpers feeling empathic to children may seek to say words that could take away the pain but in fact end up postponing grief or confusing the child's understanding of the event. *Humans don't get over a loss; they get through it.* We get through it by feeling sad, crying, being angry, talking about our feelings, nurturing ourselves or being nurtured by others, and by finding creative ways of saying goodbye in ways that feel right for us. Children need help to do this.

Helping young children with their grief

- Walk with children and allow physical action relief.
- Talk with children.
- Read children stories about loss.
- Symbolize grief and loss. Make a little garden to remember a loved one or plant a tree or shrub. 'That's Moggie's tree' (the cat).
- Put together photographs, remember them on special days and talk about them: 'Grandma would have liked to have been here today. This was her favourite tea.'

Even small losses need to be acknowledged. If we help children to cope with a small loss they will have the resources to cope with bigger losses later. Some of the losses a small child might encounter could include:

- a broken toy
- leaving an early childhood centre to start school
- loss of a pet
- moving from a cot into a bed
- giving up belongings such as a pram to a younger sibling
- losing their place at the centre of their world when a new baby comes
- taking a loved book back to the library
- having an interesting but dangerous item taken away.

We need to understand and hear small children's feelings so that they can learn to cope with these feelings. When we experience change we experience loss. It is hard to cope with too many changes and losses at one time. It helps to manage our lives, as much as possible, so that this does not happen. Children also need time to adjust to one change before coping with another.

When parents separate

Children are entitled to feel angry if their parents separate. Parents represent, often in different ways, security, love, safety and protection, and if children's love systems go into confusion and strife, they may panic, feel abandoned, insecure and anxious. If parents separate it is inevitable that children will grieve. Even a bad mother or father is the only mother or father that the child has. However, children might lose much more in the course of a separation than just their parents. They might also lose:

- their familiar home
- their bedroom
- members of their extended family
- favourite play places
- familiar routines
- their early childhood centre
- pets
- regular contact with the other parent
- a certain standard of living
- stability and permanence
- the happiness of a parent.

All children need the love, attention and modelling from parents of both sexes. If for some reason one parent is no longer available, safe substitutes of that sex ideally need to be found from among relatives and friends. The opposite sex teaches us how to respond and interact with one half of the population and future heterosexual partners. The same sex parent teaches us who we are and validates the features of our sex and gender.

Kate's husband died when her children were young. Kate took the children to swimming lessons and to gym classes and made sure that they had male coaches when possible. She also strengthened her relationship with her brother so that the children had the attention of a much-loved uncle.

Professionals assisting parents who are separating need to emphasize the importance of separated parents never talking about the other parent in a derogatory way, either in front of the children, or overhearing parents talk to other adults. Parents may not get on together but, for the welfare of their children, they need to make it as easy as possible for the child to be free to relate to both parents. Separated parents need to avoid conflict when the children are present. Children witnessing their significant adults being respectful and solving problems are given confidence that they can also solve interpersonal stress. In many countries a family court provides assistance to resolve conflict through either counselling or mediation.

Small children especially need to know that they are not responsible for the separation and they will need to be told this many times. Young children are more egocentric and see themselves at the centre of their world. Because of this, they believe that they must be responsible for what has happened as part of their survival mechanism.

Dave was in counselling. He was finding it hard to cope with his wife leaving him. He recalled that when he was four his own mother had left. 'History repeating itself', he said. 'I can still remember standing at the window and seeing her going down the path and getting into that car. I had thrown the most enormous tantrum that morning. I thought I had made her go.' Tears filled his eyes. 'I didn't make her go did I? I think that all this time somewhere inside myself I thought I did.'

We need to assist parents in helping children cope with the powerful emotions that arise at this time. Parents need to show that they think they understand how their children are feeling and they need to provide positive, appropriate ways for the children to express their feelings. Talking is best because children then learn an emotional language. Parents might try using the sharing scrapbook (see pp.104–105). Sometimes children need a way to express emotions physically (see pp.95–97).

Children may also feel angry with the parent who is the main caregiver. Sometimes a child believes that one parent is keeping her from the other parent, and she needs a chance to express those thoughts and feelings, as uncomfortable as they may be, to the caregiver. The child may also be angry with herself at times, and then feel depressed.

Each separated child needs to have her own personal space in the 'other parent's' house: a bed, a shelf or chest of drawers, complete with pictures and toys. The child can also then hold thoughts of this place in her head when she is not there. Toys sometimes assist transfer of the child from one world to another. Parents should also see that toys that came from the other house return next time to reduce any contention about origins.

Tomas had begun wetting the bed again and looking unhappy. His father found out that Tomas' bed at his mother's house was now being used by the daughter of Mum's new partner and Tomas was sleeping on a sofa.

Professional helpers can assist parents who are often self-involved to understand that the child's welfare is more important than theirs, and that parent welfare should be delayed while children need attention. Parents can help children to feel they belong in both new homes by referring to 'Dad's home and Mum's home', not 'home and your mother's place'.

Often, when parents separate, the main caregiver needs to return to full-time work. Children need even more positive attention at this time. Professional helpers need to ensure that children in their care receive a lot of individual attention and that their emotional needs are met. (See pp.135–137 on choosing a childcare placement.)

If grandparents have been part of a child's life, it is important to try to maintain this contact. One set of grandparents should not suddenly get excluded due to a blame–punishment scenario. Often children can talk to grandparents and they can provide a continuity of security at a time when a child's world may seem to be falling apart.

When working out children's access to their parents it helps to remember that children at different ages need different arrangements. A toddler will probably not cope with overnight stays away from her familiar bed, toys, bath and more constant carer. A two-year-old may cope with overnight stays but probably needs one night a week to start with. Parents need to talk through ways of maintaining the same security and order in both homes. Children should be able to have things that they find comforting in both places. These might include soft toys, a cuddly blanket, a favourite cup or a dressing gown. A common contention is the issue of different rules in different homes. Different people and different genders parent in different ways, but it is important that some agreement is held so that the transition and expectations are similar and comfortable.

When parents decide to tell the children about their separation it is better if they do it together. Children will need to know when and how they can contact the other parent. They need to know when they will be seeing the other parent. Some children like to cross off the days on the calendar. It is important that access times with the other parent are kept and that children are collected and returned as arranged. All this helps a child to feel secure and able to rebuild trust. Without this trust future relationships are threatened. Quizzing, on return, about the other parent, puts the child in a difficult position of loyalty and disclosure.

A third party, such as a counsellor or social worker may assist to ensure that special occasions and holidays are shared so that children get to celebrate with both parents.

When parents split there is a danger that a boy may be encouraged to become 'the man of the house' or a daughter take on the mother's role in taking care of the family. This can set a child up for life with these roles and lead to lifelong stress as the person continues to look after others and ignores their own needs.

Professional helpers need to watch and challenge any cases of parents who express their anger towards the other parent through the children, either by passing messages or by depriving the other of parental contact or punishing the children.

When a parent leaves a child

We may all recall experiences of being left: by a partner, a boyfriend or girlfriend, a betrayal by a friend at school, by a parent when we started school and before that, when our own parents left us to cope with the big world of early childhood, or with babysitters.

When a parent comes to leave a child at a care centre or with a caregiver often these stored experiences, memories and feelings re-emerge from memory. The 'leaving' parent usually goes into strong identification with the child. They can also add their experience of guilt and doubt about the 'leaving'. They may entangle those feelings with the child and exacerbate the process.

For the child, however, there is the possibility of feeling that one or both of the parents have gone forever. These early experiences of abandonment will depend on the level of security and attachment the child feels before and during the event. Reassurance of the impermanence of the departure is helpful in reducing fears of abandonment.

Beth was enrolling her almost two-year-old daughter at a local day care for two mornings a week so that she could have time to finish her university studies. Her student loan debt was mounting and created pressure that countered her desire to be with her child. For three weeks prior to Jemma starting, Beth took her to visit the early childhood centre and stayed with her. Beth was pleased that the day care staff were happy for this to happen. Beth played with Jemma in the sand pit and with the other activities. They sat together through the story times and joined in the singing and music making. Beth changed Jemma's nappy in the nappy changing area so that she got used to this part of day care too. When they got home they told Jemma's dad all about Jemma's experiences. Sometimes Beth left Jemma playing alongside the other children and sat back and watched. This way Jemma gradually had the experience of playing by herself. The staff related well to Jemma and included her in activities. On some visits Jemma had lunch as she would when she stayed without her mum.

On Jemma's first day alone Beth was anxious. She stayed with Jemma for half an hour before leaving. The staff encouraged Beth to say goodbye to Jemma and not sneak out as this would damage Jemma's trust. On the first morning Jemma looked puzzled when her mother left but did not cry. On the next morning, however, she became distressed. The staff comforted Jemma and Beth left feeling distressed.

A few days later, when Mum and Jemma were driving near to the day care, Jemma began to cry. 'Huggie Mummy,' she said over and over.

Beth decided to talk with the day care supervisor who suggested that Beth come early and spend some time with Jemma at the beginning of the day and that, for a few sessions, she come early to fetch Jemma and stay there while Jemma ate her lunch. Jemma's dad also managed to make some visits at around lunch time so that he, too, became part of this new aspect of Jemma's world.

After three weeks, Jemma began waking up and asking to go to her 'school'. On some occasions, when a familiar member of the day care staff was away or if Mum and Dad had been stressed at home, Jemma was unsettled. Beth knew that this was a time to stay longer with Jemma to settle her in. Sometimes the unsettled behaviour was a signal that Jemma was feeling unwell.

Here are some other ideas to help children to separate from their parents:

- Provide a small child with a tiny soft toy, 'a special friend', to keep in her pocket or a belt bag.

- Leave something that reminds a child of her mum or dad – for example, a hanky, scarf or jewellery or stone.

When Sarah left her son Andy at day care, she took with her a pair of her earrings. She showed Andy that she was putting one earring in his day care bag and one in her own handbag. 'One for you and one for me and we will put them together when I get back.'

Parents can be aware and encouraged to:

- know the people they are leaving the child with and ensure that the child knows them well too

- be attuned to the child's distress and let the child know this

- understand that children will normally be angry with the parent for leaving them

- be reassuring: 'I know it's hard for you to stay without Mummy. I will be back as soon as I can'

- begin leaving a child for a short time only at first

- remember that a young child's concept of time is different from an adult's. To the child, half an hour without parents may seem like two hours

- give the child lots of positive attention when the parent gets back

- if possible, ensure that both parents know the childcare place so that it can be talked about at home and therefore becomes part of the child's familiar world

- if a child is starting an early childhood centre, parents should try to ensure that not too many things are happening in the child's life at that time – for example, after the birth of a sibling is not a good time, or after moving house.

Some ideas that may help a carer reduce a child's anxiety and anger:

- Spend time every day with the child if you are the parent or caregiver. This may be just ten minutes at bed time to do her sharing scrapbook and read a story.

- Older children also enjoy being read to, so include older peers for a peer bonding experience.

- Be clear and firm with boundary setting (see pp.52–58).

- Give praise and encouragement when a child behaves well – for example, 'I like the way you were sharing the blocks with your brother.'

- Criticize the child's behaviour, not the child. 'I want you to stop hitting your sister' *not* 'You are a naughty boy.'

- Talk with the child about what happened in the day.

- If a child is unhappy or angry about loss or disruption in her life, listen to how she is feeling and show understanding. Parents sometimes try to explain it to make their own feelings better but the focus needs to remain on the child.

- Try holding a distraught or angry child lovingly and firmly. The security of this may be what she needs. Hold her until she calms down and resorts to crying.

- A carer's voice needs to be firm and low. Shouting winds a child up.

- If a boy has lost contact with his father (or a girl with her mother), and this cannot be restored, find a trusted same gender family friend or relative who would be willing to have regular contact with the child as a model.

- Let the child know when she will be having regular contact with her parent or caregivers – for example, 'We will sit together at bed time and talk or read every day'; 'I will come back after your lunchtime.'

- Suggest blowing bubbles, playing with water, having a bubble bath, swinging, being held, being wrapped in a cuddly blanket. Provide comforting toys.

- Find suitable energetic activities such as trampolining, climbing, running, wrestling with the father.

- Provide project opportunities to create and assemble so that the child has a feeling of achievement.

Chapter 8

Responding to Anger in Early Childhood Education and Childcare Settings

Much of the material in this book has intentionally been general, appropriate to either parents or those professionals working with children, whether at home or in a nursery setting. This chapter, however, focuses on issues particularly relevant to professionals.

Going to an early childhood centre is probably a child's first big move out into the world and away from parents. Many parents and children feel apprehensive and confused at this time; insecurity, a possible sense of abandonment and fear of the new mean that anger is closer to the surface as a response to even a mild threat.

Professionals need to be able to respond when parents ask:

- Which is the best place for my child?
- Is my child ready for this?
- How do I know if my child will be happy there?
- Will my child be safe?
- Will my child learn from this experience?
- How will my child be cared for if he gets upset?

Parents typically need to visit the centre they are considering several times before making a decision. They may ask more questions:

- What is the atmosphere like at the centre?
- Do the children seem happy?
- Is there a variety of educational toys and games?
- Is there provision for creative play such as painting?
- Do the adults get involved with the children as they play? Do they encourage them and provide good language models?

- Is there scope for active play? And are provisions for active play safe?

- Is there space for quiet times?

- How do the staff set limits for children? Are the staff firm but respectful?

- Do the staff seem happy in their work?

- Are the staff empathically sensitive to the children's needs and feelings?

- Are the children allowed to express their emotions?

- Do staff pay attention to hygiene and are the children helped to learn hygiene procedures?

- Is there a high or low staff-to-child ratio?

- Is the equipment well maintained?

- Do adults 'get down to the child's level' in their interaction?

Children under the age of three especially need a secure, available relationship with a small group of adults who are understanding and empathic and a constant feature of their lives. They need to be able to relate closely with at least one of these adults. They need to know that that person is there for them, particularly when they are distressed, but the person also needs to share their joy, pride, excitement, curiosity or love.

Between the ages of three and five children need scope for discovery, adventure, exploration learning and beginning friendships in a safe environment. They need provision for creative play and continuing language development.

Parents may hold other agendas and presuppositions as to what a good centre is and these may be neither noble, accurate nor healthy. Parents need to be aware if they are holding silently or openly some of the following thoughts:

- What is the social class of this centre?

- What is the racial and religious mix of this centre?

- Can I afford the fees?

- Will they take my child for all the hours that I need for my job?

- How will they discipline my child?

- Why is there a male worker here?

- Why do I have to go on a waiting list?

- Will they ask awkward questions about my life/partner/happiness/discipline?

- Can they handle my child, because the last place couldn't?

- Can they fix my child's problems?

Professional caregivers need to have answers for these questions that will be as diverse as the people asking them. Experienced workers may encourage disclosure of such questions, the parent's doubts and hidden agendas by using the following questions:

'Were you worried about the number of [type of] children here?'

'Is the Christian ethos held at the centre okay with you?'

'We don't hit children but we do take children into isolation to protect others. Is that okay with you?'

Changing centres is an upheaval for the child, not to mention the other children experiencing their departures and arrivals, so it is best to get things out in the open before entry. Declining a client may even be an option if it means a child does not have to be uprooted later on. Centres with a strong business model and values may need to consider that quality, stability and long-term wellbeing have their own reward, and ultimately will raise the reputation and therefore the business popularity.

A useful tactic is to have a set of maybe 10 to 20 information sheets available for all new parents outlining the centre's policy, routines, expectations of parents, suggestions for particular problems (for example, 'Things you may need to know if you are separating'; 'Why violence in the family is not good for anyone' etc.), values and recommendations (for example, 'Keep fathers involved'). Parents then know where they stand, you know where you stand, and you can draw parents back to the sheets at appropriate times with a gentle re-issue of the forms. Some centres even ask for a signature to show that the parents understand the rules set, so these do not come into dispute.

Care and education centres should require parents to be part of ongoing activities, and one of these should be ongoing parental education. This moves the enquiring parent away from the notion that the centre is a convenient 'dumping ground' with business anonymity, and that they can expect a more holistic approach to their family wellbeing.

Anger in the early years environment

Early childhood professionals are increasingly experiencing what they perceive as an increase in anger levels and an increase in aggressive behaviour, particularly behaviour that threatens or damages others. They are rightly concerned as we all have a commitment to keep children, ourselves and our property safe.

Reports of anger and aggressive behaviour are becoming more common in early childhood centres and are a growing concern to educators and caregivers.

Children never feel angry for no reason, so we can assume that any or all of the following are happening:

- Children have more to feel angry about.
- Society is condoning more aggressive and abusive behaviour.
- Children feel less restricted in early childhood centres and are engaging in more expressive behaviour.

It may well be that they are all true and to some extent the care centre, nursery, playcentre or playgroup may be reflecting such changes.

Children have more to feel angry about

Deprivation is worth feeling angry about

Much has been made in past decades of overt abuse. What is more difficult to name and deal with is the lack of attention to a child's developmental and relational needs – this is covert abuse, negligence or unintended neglect and deserves as much attention.

Relational bonds

The 'deal' for children has changed greatly over the last 50 years. Children are no longer guaranteed personal, one-on-one care for the first five years of their lives. While day care centres have tried to supply the highest possible standard of care, it is clear that this must be balanced with solid attachment to the parent/s or primary caregiver that is based on sufficient time for strong, constant attachment to take place. It is also clear from recent research, especially from the attachment theorists, that securely attached children do well in early childhood and later in life, and that ambivalent and avoidant attachment is associated with problems that include insecurity, anger and aggression (Belsky 2002; Cline 1979; Coen 2011). While some childcare centres will certainly dispute this, children who spend more than 20 hours a week in care have been clearly identified as prone to ambivalent and avoidant attachment, and thus anger-based or insecure behaviour.

This is not to suggest that childcare centres are not doing their best to satisfy a demand for quality services within competitive budgets. It may, however, beg the question of whose needs are being met: the child's needs or the parents' need to work full time. Children need stable, responsible, loving childcare and nearly all parents want to do the very best for their children. However, some parents may need to rethink their priorities and be clear about the child's developmental needs and whether these needs are being traded off against other needs, such as maintaining a certain 'standard of living'. Another consequence of this trading off is a sense of guilt and a 'making up' to the child by the parents – many working parents compensate for their absence and want the home time to be 'happy time'. They may then fail to discipline children and give them firm, consistent boundaries. Maintaining clear boundaries, even when the time parents have with their child(ren) is constrained by working arrangements, is essential to their sense of order and security. Professional helpers may also need to deal with hyper-advocacy from parents as a sign, mainly to themselves, that they truly care about their children. Professionals can play an important role in providing advice and guidance about the developmental needs of babies and young children so that parents can make informed decisions within the context of their particular circumstances.

Where a child's developmental and relational needs are not being met, the child will feel anxious and stressed and move to anger as a defence, crying for attention at the deprivation or powerlessness.

Increasingly the assumption that a child will live with two committed parents is no longer valid. There is, however, no reason that children cannot have two parents living separately who are both committed and involved. What may prevent this are parents who have unresolved differences and who continue to fight. This is disturbing and confusing for children and selfish on behalf of the parents who do so in a manner that conveys conflict and hostility to the child, generally in a covert manner. Additionally, the custodial parent may control and prevent the full participation of the non-resident parent. This, too, can be devastating and holds the children in a powerless turmoil. This is good reason for the child to feel angry.

Child abuse

It is the social and parental responsibility of adults to use their power to protect children. This power can sometimes also be misused, resulting in a child's needs being neglected or a child being abused.

Child abuse may be in the form of overt physical, verbal, relational, emotional or sexual abuse, but may also be unintended, as in the case of some neglect. Abuse is monitored and nations are challenged by the UN Convention on the Rights of the Child through a committee that visits signatory nations every five years and reports on how they measure up. Although children may be expressing their distress at abuse more openly and it is likely that more sensitized professionals and communities are noticing it, most abuse is still not reported.

Children remain the most unprotected group of people in our community. The physical hitting of adult people and most animals is banned in most Western nations, but not so for children (World Health Organization 2002). Fortunately, there is a move in an increasing number of countries to make it illegal for parents and caregivers to use physical punishment.

We need to notice children's anger and respond to it. Anger is always a response to some form of powerlessness. Children's anger may therefore result from an overt action or an act of conscious or unconscious negligence. An angry child requires respect and investigation, not silencing, distraction or avoidance. The small voice needs to be heard.

Society is condoning more aggressive and abusive behaviour

The increased competition in our society since the mid-1980s has meant that stress levels, for most people, have gone up. A less equal distribution of global and national wealth means that more people are missing out on 'fair shares' (Wilkinson and Pickett 2009). People are resorting to more competitive or desperate measures and this includes crime, aggression and dishonesty. The greatest correlation of violence to any other causal factor is the association between violence and unequal distribution of wealth. An increase in violence is directly associated with an increase in difference between those who are rich and those who are poor. Children then are more exposed to community and family violence and have a reduced sense of safety.

Children are witnessing more violence and abuse on television and in films. Television cartoons have up to three times the incidence of violence as compared with adult programmes (Bridgman 1998). Our homes use more security technology. The use of violence will inevitably be evident in our early childhood centres due to this, as children respond to surrounding models.

Children feel less restricted in early childhood centres and are engaging in more expressive behaviour

Preschool centres should be safe places for children to express emotion. However, this means that teachers and caregivers end up picking up more pieces from other people's lives and their parent/counsellor role has increased. But if we stress that anger is an emotion and as such needs expression like any other emotion, we should view the expression of anger as useful and healthy. Recall also that anger is quite normal and is not abuse. What is of concern is *how* anger is expressed in early childhood centres. Abuse and violence are behaviours that should never be tolerated in an institution or centre regardless of the child's distress. Many educators and caregivers put up with behaviour and abuse that would be a crime if the perpetrator was an adult. Professionals should not have to tolerate abuse, verbal or physical, from any child. Such early childhood professionals have a good opportunity to regulate and stop abuse from happening at an early age.

Exercise: An approach to attention-seeking, destructive behaviour

For attention-seeking, destructive behaviour, when the child arrives at the centre, arrange to have four appointments of 'noticing' the child. That means that you arrange a time to visit, connect, sit and affirm the child during the session. After the first appointment say, 'I will come and see you again soon and find out what great work you are doing.'

Keep tightly to the appointments and times so a secure, reliable pattern is established.

Deliberate, positive 'noticing' can replace negative attention seeking, and it can be reduced in frequency and time. Sometimes, however, even conscientious and caring workers may end up working in a way that doesn't help the child, and this can contribute to a child's anger levels. Here is a list of 'Do's and Don't's:

- *Don't rationalize that 'they are little so it doesn't matter'.* Little assaults hurt little people, and little assaults turn into big assaults. Professional educators report that they have been kicked, bitten and spat at, but avoid being reactive and instead are compassionate: 'He's only three'; 'He seems so upset about something.' However, it is not right to let the behaviour go unaccounted for. This is an opportunity to teach and direct in the early years so that major pain and destruction can be avoided in later years when such behaviour is unacceptable in adulthood.

- *Do hold abusive action accountable and create consequences that will deter it.* After the behaviour is addressed, then is the time for compassion and listening to the child's vulnerable feelings, and giving hope for tears, not violence.

- *Don't ignore the behaviour and hope it will go away because it is 'attention seeking'.* You will have noticed it so you are not completely ignoring it. It sets a norm for the future that it is possible to do things and not get reactions. The child is seeking attention, and positive attention needs to be given, not condoning by avoidance.

- *Do plan attention times.* This may need to be initially multiple 'attention visits' at regular intervals, and can be reduced in frequency as a child feels more secure or important.

- *Do teach a child to ask for help.* This requires that the child be aware of need and feels that you are interested enough to give attention when contact is made. Parents dismissing a child or promising an eternal 'later' may wonder where they went wrong when their adolescent chooses peers to share problems with.

A constructive approach to aggressive or destructive acts needs to cover the following:

- Stop violence by setting clear boundaries and consequences, and having consistent, appropriate responses. The behaviour must be addressed first and its expression called to account. Better expression can be taught or shown. Withdrawal with an adult companion may be needed for calming and consequence.

- Listen to the child's anger with full attention and empathy. There is a good reason why the child feels angry. Listen, validate and dissipate the charge.

- Track back with the child to the vulnerable emotions behind the anger and put words to the emotions if needed. Identify the cause of the powerlessness.

- Strategize to put the situation right and ensure that the child's needs and rights are met. This may involve bridging through to home and the care centre and winning the parents' co-operation and insight to reduce the child's distress if that is the origin. It may be as simple as helping get some coloured pens back from a peer.

- Establish yourself as a trusted adult who can be relied on to pay attention to the child's issues. This will increase attunement and a sense of care. It may also involve coaching a parent in the above procedure and in how to increase care, responsiveness and attachment.

Attachment, childcare and parental bonds

One other issue that should at least be raised in any chapter on childcare in relation to anger and children is the issue of attachment, and whether formal childcare arrangements can have an impact upon relational bonds.

As a general rule, the more love and attention a child receives from parents within a boundaried setting, the less anger, stress and anti-social reaction they will have later. Research is currently showing us that solid bonding and attachment in the first three years is needed for secure and happy children (Ainsworth and Salter 2010; Ainsworth *et al.* 1978; Belsky 2002; Karen 1990a). That means that more than 20 hours' a week childcare may not be good for children (Belsky 2002) (see pp.13–15). Naturally, it is beyond the ability of childcare providers to dictate terms, and it is not our intention to lecture parents on the number of hours their children are cared for, but it is worth being aware of this research, as it may have some bearing in relation to a child's subsequent behaviour.

Many nursery teachers have reported increased difficulty with children's anger and aggression. Theory and research suggests that there could be long-term problems for these children (Belsky 2002; Lawson 2008; NICHD ECCRN 2001; Pace and Zappulla 2010). It is essentially from an attachment bond that people learn to relate in an empathic, intimate way. The bonding between parents and child, and the sense of a constant, caring interaction with the child on a one-on-one basis, is very important to the young child's security and ability to socialize. It gives a base of security, love, worthiness and confidence that will last for the rest of their lives.

> The more time children spend in any kind of non-maternal care across the infant, toddler and early childhood years, the more aggressive and disobedient they were at four or higher, according to caregivers in childcare, and at kindergarten age, and according to mothers and teachers. (Belsky 2002, p.167)

> Children with greater exposure to non-maternal care during the first 4.5 years of life were rated by their pre-school and kindergarten teachers as more aggressive, assertive and defiant than same-age children with less exposures. (Dworkin, cited in Belsky 2002, p.167)

Opposing views

Critics of attachment theory suggest that it does not consider the power and effectiveness of the extended family to childcare with trusted people. This argument may have some substance, although attachment theory did originate from studying African extended families. Most researchers would consider that extended families have attachment problems if there is no core attachment figure (Brandell and Ringel 2007).

The issue of income is sometimes argued as important for the standard of living of the modern nuclear family. Questions must arise, however, as to the values being used which appear to put wealth and assets above relationships and children.

This is clearly a difficult and emotive subject, and one to be broached very carefully. It is clear, however, that as part of emotional and relational security, children need to attach and bond to an adult in a constant, loving manner, especially in the first three to five years when they are learning so much about trust and empathy (although attachment is important at all ages). Failure to do this brings social and intergenerational problems of relating empathically (Feeney 1999; Lawson 2008; Main et al. 1985; Meyers and Landsberger 2002; Pace and Zappulla 2010). So, we believe that formal childcare is best kept to no more than 20 hours a week after the child has reached the age of three, and caregiving is best done by the mother, father or a single regular caregiver prior to that age. We cannot support the notion that multiple carers with multiple charges can meet the child's needs before that age. There are even commentators who consider there should be no childcare other than the parents or a constant, individual caregiver before the age of three (Biddulph 2003).

Early childhood educators working with parents

The next chapter goes into much more detail about parents, the role of parenting in relation to anger in early childhood, and how to help to support parents. Here are some suggestions specific to early years childcare settings for how to approach the difficult task of addressing the issue with parents when a child is unhappy or engaging in anti-social behaviour.

- Have a list of referral agencies and services to give all clients on entry so that they can seek help themselves.

- Run education evenings at the centre on the topics that you think are needed, ensuring first of all that certain parents are available and willing.

- Run a children's anger evening for parents.

- Take one parent aside and have an informal chat to see if he or she is comfortable speaking to you about the child.

- Do initial engagement interviews with the parents in their home.

- Show a list of expectations for parents and ask them to agree to them before enrolling their child at the centre.

- Show a list of difficulties and reasons why children feel angry before starting at the centre and ask if the child has any of these reasons or difficulties. The child may have several, and the question then is how the child is handling the issue.

- Use the 'Working out a plan' exercise (see pp.81–83) with the parent.

- Explain that children are never angry for no reason.

- Have a bottom line as to when a family is excluded; this usually relates to the safety of the other children.

- Ignore attention seeking if it seems useful to do this.

- Invite the parents to sit in at a distance and be unnoticed.

- Invite parents to sit and assist their child.

- Speak in terms of 'WE have a problem', so they feel less like they are being attacked.

- Explain how difficult some of the child's behaviour may be for you as a concerned and committed carer.

- Arrange behaviour reporting.
- Set up a mentor for the child.
- If you suspect the child has been abused, follow your establishment's procedures and local and national guidance.
- Arrange a family meeting and watch the dynamics of the family.

Check the following factors as they consistently show in referrals to support services:

- Does the child lack a sufficient number of parents (see pp.176–177)?
- Does the child *not* have the birth father living with him?
- Has the child spent long hours in childcare?
- Is the child going to further care somewhere else?
- Has the child suffered abuse or is he still suffering abuse?
- Has the child suffered trauma or loss in his lifetime?

It is possible to get support, remedial action, intervention or assistance for any of the above.

CHECKLIST FOR EARLY CHILDHOOD CENTRES (YES/NO COMMENTS)

- Is it okay to have a child in your centre who feels angry?
- What do you do with a child who hurts others?
- What do you do with a child who hurts you?
- How do you create and use time out (for example, Time Out Chair, special room, expressing place, calming place)?
- How do you raise a child's anti-social behaviour issues with parents?
- Do you have a plan of action for dealing with exceptional violence/abuse?
- What do you have in the child's environment to help with anger?
- How do you model dealing with your own anger at work?
- Do you have a baseline of ethics/requirements from the parents and/or the children for entry? What does it include?
- How clear are your centre's boundaries? What are they? How are they maintained?

Try taking some of the questions that may be unanswered to a staff or association meeting.

The Anger Rules

ANGER RULES

It's okay to feel angry BUT:

- Don't hurt others.
- Don't hurt yourself.
- Don't hurt property.
- Do talk about it.

The Anger Rules are an excellent boundary-setting exercise for any group or care home or centre. They can be presented as a poster, bookmark, drawing or information technology (IT) message. They are easily remembered and are often reported as being a reminder that has saved a child or adult from hurting another or oneself.

The advantages of the Anger Rules are that:

- they are clear and impart values
- they are boundary setting
- they are short and to the point
- children remember them and can tell you them.

Teaching the rules to an adult or child:

- Go through the rules one line at a time. Explain the concepts.
- *'It's okay to feel angry'* is the most important, but there needs to be a clear boundary to the anger and that is best described as being *inside* the body. Anything outside the body is a behaviour and behaviours can be okay or not okay (see pp.89–90).
- *'Don't hurt others.'* This includes physical, mental/emotional, verbal, sexual and spiritual hurt. Be clear that physical hurting is only one sort of hurting.
- *'Don't hurt yourself.'* This means in any of the above ways, including putting yourself in danger.

- *'Don't hurt property.'* This means damaging, stealing, losing, not returning, tagging, hiding or defacing property.

- *'Do talk about it.'* This is the positive that balances the three negatives, and is the most effective way of expressing anger to get what you want.

- Ask the parents or child (if he is old enough) to repeat the Anger Rules. Spot-check the rules. Write them down, form them in clay or solid media, use the Anger Rules poster, draw yourself saying it to someone, act out saying it in a role-play, shout it, whisper it, remind each other, sing it to others. Have the parent explain why this is a good idea.

- Keep the written rules on the wall so that they are always visual to the class or the child.

- Acknowledge them in an institutional setting so that it is part of the education culture.

- Have competitions for who can say them in the quickest, slowest, most excited, most boring, saddest or happiest way.

In an education setting, the Anger Rules could be applied in the following ways:

- They should be displayed in as many places as possible in the community, and sent home – they give a clear message to parents of values held outside of the home.

- Vary the size range from poster size to the size of an exercise book or even a card that is carried like a credit card.

- Teach them to all teaching/caring staff, parents, visitors and new children as base values and behaviour expectations.

- They are a starting place with a child when discussing behaviour: 'Have you kept the Anger Rules?'; 'What are they?'

- They can be learned by recitation and memorizing with children given a reward when a class or person is asked to demonstrate them.

- Even if a person/parent does not initially believe in them, by learning them it does seem to change that thinking.

Chapter 9

Understanding the Influence of Parents and Parenting

Professional helpers are often faced with questions from parents about children's behaviour and emotions. Most of the time parents are doing it right, and just need affirmation and encouragement. While strengths-based encouragement and positive affirmation is an important part of building up parents and carers, sometimes it is important to also assist them by recognizing parenting patterns that are not useful, and encouraging different approaches. Helping professionals are in a position to assist that process.

Wanting their children to like them

Parents need to be adult enough to not need to have their children like them all of the time. Parents need to *not need* their children. They need to like themselves enough to be able to ensure that a child does things when the child may not want to, and be strong should the child get angry or even hostile. The parent or caregiver needs to have another adult person who likes and supports them, not the child – it is not a child's job to support the parent's self-esteem and to give the parent love. It *is*, however, the parent's job to do that for the child. Parents who *depend* on their child will be manipulated and may wonder why they have poor respect and behaviour management. The child also risks becoming co-dependent, role-confused, resentful, deprived of childish, unconditional trust and ultimately resents the parent.

Parents need to act and know that *they will not be liked by their child all the time and that is okay. It may even be a good sign.* Sometimes a child will say that they 'hate you', that you are a 'bad parent' or that they will 'run away'. This is likely to be because the parent's care and concern has limited their freedom. We have to teach children how to use freedom but at times protect them until they have the awareness and skills to act for themselves.

Giving assistance

All adults need adult affirmation. It threatens our mental health if we do not have this. Professional helpers should work with the parent to ascertain and develop such support. These may be tender questions as the parent realizes and acknowledges that they feel alone and are sad about that. These two things should be checked:

- *Are they really alone?* Often there are parents of the parent, the other parent of the child, friends or neighbours who would easily help, support and befriend, but the client parent has either become estranged or is ashamed to ask for help. There may be a reply of 'But they don't care'; 'They are too busy'; 'I don't get on.' The 'don't care' and 'too busy' reply is usually the result of poor self-esteem and a lack of self-worth, and when broken through it is frequently the case that others do care, and would give time even if they were busy. The 'I don't get on' reply is worth examining. Often it is because of a past dispute, or dislike of a characteristic. Conflict resolution is often easier if there is a challenge of 'Would you be prepared to let go/settle the upset for the sake of your child?' Most people will do anything if they see that it is for the better wellbeing of their child.

- If there is no support then the question becomes, *who could provide support and how can this be established?* Social clubs, interest or education groups, sport, culture, neighbourhood watch are all places of common interest for the most unlikely of individuals. Childcare networks can give valuable time to release from the grind of meeting children's needs. The internet and cheap telephone technology enable people to communicate on a scale that previously was unimaginable. Skyping, social networks and blogging allow unprecedented meeting and sharing; however, parent and play groups remain the best place to talk to each other and feel better about the trials of parenting, and are probably the best source of relevant and immediate support. The position that parents need adult affirmation, love and respect is not negotiable.

Wanting their child to be happy all the time

Some parents feel bad if their child is in any way uncomfortable or experiencing upset or vulnerability, but we simply can't take away, nor should we try to take away, a child's upset and vulnerable feelings. It is best that the child feels them and learns how to deal with them, as long as the child is safe to do so. Our care and concern are usually more based on, and about, preventing some things that happened to *us* as children. Parents who need their child to be happy all the time may feel manipulated, and have poor routines and discipline. And the child will have diminishing respect for them, becoming more demanding. Often such parents feel guilty about their parenting because they feel in some way that they are not doing what a good parent should.

The most common situation is the working parent who wants it all to be roses when they come home at the end of the day. This is difficult when the child wants to express their anger at the small amount of bonding time that they may have with Mum or Dad, or the way they are moved around between carers. And they have a right to that anger. Sometimes a parent tries to look for alternative sources for those 'not good' feelings, and consequently puts responsibility on others outside the home. For instance, early childhood educators often report children who are unappreciative and ego-centred and held back in empathy development. The discomfort of working with such children comes from first experiencing the child's anger transferred onto them and then the pattern of 'it's your job to make me happy' played out in care settings.

Giving assistance

The parent needs to allow the child to experience fear, unhappiness, sadness, hurt and worry for periods of time, as long as the child is safe. The parent's task is to provide safety, love, soothing and hope. It is much safer if the child learns to cope at this age with those feelings rather than later as an adult or adolescent when their support is not around. Assist the child to problem solve. Help them to come up with ideas for fixing things, or ways of bringing back the good feelings. Then help them implement the solution.

Shifting the child's brain hemispheres from feeling to thinking is essential learning. Total parental rescuing shortcuts this and reduces personal responsibility for the action, making it someone else's responsibility to solve the child/person's problem. Many adults are unable to shift from 'child-like helplessness', and end up waiting for a 'parental rescue' from others.

Problem-solving questions may include approaches such as:

'That's terrible. [empathy] What could we do to put that right? [plan]'

'Sounds like that really hurt. [feeling behind the anger is acknowledged] How can I help you so that doesn't happen again? [plan]'

'I'd be angry too if that happened to me. [validation of anger] What do you want us to do? [plan]'

Being afraid that others will think that they are bad parents

Sometimes parents behave in certain ways or demand that their children act in certain ways so that others will think good of them and like them. Parenting must always be for the long-term good of the child, not a performance. The desire to look like a good parent is shame-based. The key factor is the shame that the parent or caregiver feels when in public or in front of friends or other parents – for example, at a parent playgroup.

Young children have a sensitive nose for the parent who wants to look good. They know immediately the power they have in that situation, to behave in ways that they may never have done before. 'He's not like this at home'; 'I don't believe she said/did that' may be their response to observers. Children quickly sense when you are weak in front of someone or something and play with that powerlessness in you.

The classic is the supermarket tantrum. Mum or Dad are in public and suddenly lose their normal responses, such as threatening a consequence, or having a growl, because it doesn't look good, and instead whisper vicious threats into the child's ear. The child gets the *hidden* aspect of the anger and shame and plays into it with more bad behaviour, demands and maybe even a tantrum. Hassling a parent when they are engaged in a telephone conversation is another discovery of a weak or 'embarrassment' spot and could be an opportunistic attempt to push a boundary or get a 'goodie' that would be harder to get under usual circumstances. The parent's anger or embarrassment is hidden and played on.

Giving assistance

Fixing this one is about being able to recognize shame and embarrassment and mindfully catch a moment of recognition that this is what is being played with. The solution is devilishly simple. A self-affirmation that you know that you are a good parent and then interrupting the *public* dynamic is the solution. Saying 'I'm sorry I have to deal with something' and then behaving in a normal, consistent manner, such as hiding the biscuit box they brought to you on the phone, or taking the child who is having a tantrum to the car away from the public scenario, breaks the shame effect.

Or, quite simply, confidently reassuring oneself with the mantra, 'Do what you know is best, and don't put on acts for others.'

Being too reasonable

It is very important for parents to respect the child and consider their feelings. However, there is a point at which the parent makes a judgement that, for the good and wellbeing of the child, the child's reasons and feelings will be overridden. This takes place due to the adult's maturity and wisdom and their judgement that the parents' reasons, which are based on safety, risk assessment and knowledge of skill and development, are more important than the child's opinion and feeling at this time.

Overly 'reasonable' parents may be so thoughtful and empathize so well that they put the child's thoughts and reasons before their own, often due to an uncertain sense of themselves and a desire to be the 'best' parent for the child. Understanding the child's reasons is very important, but when it comes to safety and care, the caring parent should have both experience and perspective to make a loving decision based on the bigger picture. Doing up the child's car safety belt, although she may protest and say that she doesn't like to be confined, is an example of the greater knowledge of the parent overriding the child, her reasons and her anger. The loving parent has the big picture and the child doesn't (see more on 'the big picture' on pp.80–83).

Giving assistance

Parents need to know that it is their job to consider the bigger picture, then to decide what is best. They then need to be able to resist 'folding' when faced with the child's anger at not having their immediate, short-term, 'small picture' perspective attended to. Withdrawal of immediate empathy for the non-gratification upset is replaced by longer-term empathy for the child's future wellbeing.

Steps are:

1. Sit with the child's hurt and acknowledge it.

2. Tell the child the reason, even though she may not be able to understand.

3. Don't give in.

4. Reassure yourself of the good you are doing for your child.

Think about the importance of establishing the necessity for this by considering yourself prohibiting alcohol consumption by a 12-year-old. The 12-year-old needs to have a history of knowing that they have parents who care enough about them to prohibit and control when there is risk. The lesson for the child is, 'Although I feel angry at my parents and it's really annoying that they care about me that much and I will still kick against it, it's so nice to feel important and loved that much.'

Being over-controlling

Sometimes parents over-control the child in a manner that squashes or limits the child's sense of adventure and exploration. This may affect the child by:

- generating fear of the world
- creating dependence on the parent and reducing independence
- reducing imagination
- reducing initiative
- generating a model of control of others and the environment
- reducing resilience
- reducing spontaneity and life force
- increasing adaption to external environments rather than authentic action.

Such parents may act from either their own fear of life or a belief that all child and adult behaviour needs strong, regulatory control. Children need to have some freedom to experience decision making, a sense of curiosity, how to handle impulses and how to solve problems and develop independence. Over-control that squashes the child's initiative and sense of self fails to fulfil the original good intention of care, protection and development, damaging spontaneity and spirit.

Young children who are in a formative process will naturally experience frustration as a response to any control, as do most people when they witness freedoms being curtailed. There is a gentle balance that needs to be managed, between freedom and selfhood, and over-control, entrapment and stifling of our life force. This balance should be managed not by fear, but by learning through experience that allows a self-generated assessment of consequence and effect that is appropriate to the developmental age.

Giving assistance

Assisting parents to loosen up can be brought about by:

- education: understanding the importance of exploration and play to learning
- assisting adults to notice that their own past may be being projected onto their own child and demonstrating that times and contexts are different
- showing other examples of freedom and adventure that have been successful
- modelling fostering adventure and imagination in a safe and exciting environment
- modelling care and education that enjoys noise, excitement and robust play.

Children who are constantly restricted and limited have good reason to feel angry and may choose to act out that frustration, especially when they see other children enjoying it. In such cases parents should be invited to consider that over-regulation and control is causal to the anger being expressed and invite, 'What if...?' questions.

In summary: parents or caregivers or professional helpers should be invited to nurture spiritedness, not stifle it, squashing the child's love of life and excitement.

Using unreasonable control due to anger originating elsewhere

Some parents feel an inner urge to punish, be mean, over-control, be hard and critical. They may find that they are thinly disguising feelings of anger and act as if they are attacking the child.

The effect on the child is one of resentment that cannot be expressed as it is too dangerous, a harbouring of a grudge, a reduction of joy and spirit and a living in fear and apprehension, reduced self-esteem and a sense of seeking payback when they are older, which they usually do destructively in the teen years. Such children have a right to feel angry in the present, and have that anger heard and acted on. Professionals are usually in the position of having first contact with the child where the child may be acting out in a place that is safer to display their hurt and pain than home.

Giving assistance

The parent's anger usually comes from somewhere else and it is the professional helper's task, if using a family or dyadic systemic model, to assist the parent to track down the discontent that is being acted out inappropriately on the child. Justifications of: 'It never did me any harm'; 'The kid deserves it'; 'I have feelings too'; or 'Life's not fair so learn it now' should all be challenged for their rationale and appropriateness.

The original problem may well lie in the parent/caregiver's childhood and may well be acted out in the next generation. Access to an opportunity to work with this is usually limited, and the adult is often well defended psychologically. Innocent questions, naive comments and indirect questions can ease through the parent's defences as direct assertion often fails. Referral to professional help, such as psychotherapy and psychological enquiry, are ideal if the adult can be encouraged to attend.

The parent may feel jealous of the child, frustrated at a sense of entrapment in a caregiving role or have their anger displaced from other work or family problems and drop this on the child. Providing seminars or workshops that address these issues by a care or education agency can assist recognition of such sources. For example, a playgroup may invite a local psychologist to talk to an evening group about 'parental stress'. Nurseries sometimes keep generic handouts on a multitude of topics and give them out at opportune points, such as enrolment, seminars or even times of crisis.

Support for children suffering a punitive environment is sometimes the only option and this may be ongoing due to the continuance of the cause. Professionals must track down the source of the child's anger or assist the child to talk either directly or indirectly (through drawing or role-play).

Generally, action involves:

- Challenging abuse and reporting it where it is severe and breaks the law.

- Educating as to the consequences of the behaviour on the child and the child's future.

- Understanding the parent's hurt and struggle and showing empathy and understanding for the parent's vulnerability (not aggression). There should be no support for any rationalisation of the abuse.

- Listing the meanness and punishment that the parent endured in their own childhood, showing the parent empathy.

- Asking: Did they like it? How did they feel when it happened? Inviting consideration of what the parent's own parent could have done better. 'What would you have liked your parents to have done when…?' Turning that around on the parent as an adult switches the empathy to their child.

In summary: children respect fairness and need positivity, and parents need to deal with their own problems, not pass them on to their children.

Being unable to handle a child's anger

Some parents respond to a child's expressed anger by shouting it down or telling the child:

'Don't get angry with me.'

'You are angry. Go to your room.'

'I don't like anger.'

'We don't have anger in this house.'

These are 'It's not okay to feel or express anger' messages, and they are not useful. All children feel angry from time to time. It is normal and helps us put things right when they have gone wrong. Children's anger doesn't mean a challenge to the current power or authority, and nor does it necessarily mean a criticism of the listener. It means that something is wrong in the child's view of the world. Children are entitled to feel angry and show this without hurting anyone or being hurt by anyone.

It is our job to quietly listen (as professional helpers, parents or educators). If the child is not listened to, then that action is devaluing and risks the child deciding not to talk about it. This accentuates the likelihood of the child internalizing the issue. The alternatives are then the child taking the matter aggressively into her own hands or resigning to hopelessness.

Giving assistance

- Assist parents or carers to deal with their own fear of anger. Review why that may be and assist a decision to listen safely to the child; there should be an understanding that anger is okay.

- Clarify that a child expressing anger to a person does not mean that the anger is aimed at that person.

- Clarify that there is no need for time out or 'going to your room' unless there is a danger that someone will be hurt, which is unlikely if a child is able to talk about it.

- Thank the child for letting you know all about her angry feelings.

- Explain the consequences of not listening: a sense of devaluing, reduced trust, reduced intimacy, increased lack of safety for the child, carrying internalized burdens, shame.

- Learn 'empathic noises' skills, and the shifting of understanding to the child's perspective.

In summary: listen to the child's anger.

Being too busy

The decision by most parents to have two full-time paid providers leaves a potential relational gap for the child. Given the need for attachment in the early years, it takes skilful planning and parenting to achieve both full-time work and full relational attachment with their children. Sometimes parents may just fail to realize that they are not putting adequate time into their children – work is the biggest killer of family relationships, followed by a preoccupation with doing things for oneself when with a child. Leaving the children in the car while doing a task or being preoccupied with answering a mobile phone while in the middle of a conversation with a child, these are all ways of being 'too busy'. Parents who are too busy to spend the time needed by a child to feel bonded and secure and worthy should understand that their child has a good reason for feeling angry and that the adult may be resistant to hearing that.

Rationalizations are usually used to deal with any discomfort with one's busyness:

'I can give my child a better standard of living.'

'I'm not really working.'

'They have good care.'

'She [the child] doesn't seem to mind.'

'If I don't do this, I can't spend time with them later.'

'Work makes me a more interesting parent.'

'As long as [she/he] is with me it doesn't matter what I do.'

'He's so active he needs peers and a good play environment.'

'She's bored being at home with me.'

Giving assistance

Such rationalizations can usually be challenged quite easily with logic or basic values. What is really important? Quality of parenting or more money and goodies?

Rationalizations can also be challenged by education. Many parents do not have a good knowledge of developmental needs or behavioural causes that are not immediate, signs of distress, effects of stress or displaced anger. Childcare and education centres should engage parents in parent education that covers behaviour and its causes.

In summary: parents need to spend uninterrupted and devoted time with their children so that the children feel loved, connected and noticed daily. Children feel cheated and angry if they don't.

Needing to grow up

It takes adults to bring up a child, and children are entitled to expect adults to be a safe container to bring them through to independence. Some adults, however, want to be the child, and may even resent having children because it means that they haven't got their partner to themselves. This usually comes from adults having incomplete childhoods and a lack of a proper transition to adulthood. I often say to men who are considering a relationship or living with a woman who has children, 'Know this, that you need to accept that you will be number two in line after the kids. And it should be like that, because kids need first care because they are children. If you can't handle that then don't get together, or expect to be disappointed, and have tension with the kids as your competitors.' Parents that haven't grown up themselves may end up competing with their children, or they are so busy 'having fun' that the children have to try and bring themselves up.

Giving assistance

Having adults who are strong and secure, even if this may sometimes be an act, is important for child security and for the child's freedom to be a child. Therapeutic approaches include:

- Parental deficits being made up through the use of a therapist.
- Having couples talk of how they are experiencing the demands of the other. 'Giver' and 'taker' terms could be used.
- Advice and coaching on how to give (supplying need) rather than take (requiring your needs to be met). Identifying a person's 'giving' spheres and their 'taking' spheres as separate and concentrating on a balance and structure to deliver those needs – for example, child caring is a 'giving' sphere and that is what you do without expectation of return. Having a massage by a partner is a 'taking' sphere. Listening to a favourite piece of music is a 'me-time' or 'taking' sphere. These need to be in balance.

In summary: be the adult and allow the child to depend on you. Take separate time to have fun or to be a child somewhere else.

Poor stress management

All adults and children have some stress. It is extremely useful for getting tasks done, for getting out of trouble and for being an achiever. However, stress that has got too much to be useful and that has begun a reduction in accomplishment needs to be monitored and actively reduced. People become more self-centred as the stress increases, and are more likely to act *not in* empathy with others. People are more likely to access anger as a protection mechanism if they are feeling stressed.

We all have to learn how to deal with stress, both adults and children, but given the difference in power between a child and a caregiver, it is very important that *we*, the adults, have good stress management.

Giving assistance

The suggestions below can easily be done with children under the age of five as well as adults:

- Identify stressors.

- Identify personal stress indicators and point to a place on your body: 'Where does it feel upset?' (see pp.89–93).

- Check when disruptions and unhappiness happen in the child's life.

- Improve the client's mindfulness: 'Stop, breathe, notice situation and feelings, don't judge, act for all.' Help the client in looking at a stress management model and teach calming, emotional management and breathing techniques.

- Many adults need to realize that they don't have to control things as much as they thought. Active recognition of moments when you want to control, organize, dictate, guide and direct others should be recognized and 'released'. Questions around 'What if X did something different? What would happen to you?' usually uncover that there would be little or no benefit from controlling, and maybe even some benefit in not controlling. For a child: 'That's okay. David is allowed to do that. Everyone is allowed to do that. You can do that', assists a development from an ego-centred two-year-old position to a more social one.

- Generate choices. Generating options and assisting good choices is empowering in that it reduces a panic/survival response and a sense of being trapped. Choices for a toddler can also be equivalent to useful distractions.

In summary: assist the parent to show the calmness and security that they want their children to have.

Difficulties engaging emotionally with children

Much of early childhood is about learning that you, the child, are not the centre of the universe and that there are (unfortunately) others who have expectations, needs and demands that have to be accommodated along with yours. Managing impulse is an important part of that. Parents and caregivers are vital models for such emotional management. When parenting, however, as models that avoid that same self-centredness, it is important to realize that children's emotions need attention and adults' emotions can be dealt with after, because adults have better developed skills for deferring desires and needs, and better skills for strategizing on how to get them.

Giving assistance

Children live with more immediacy. We need to engage with them now at the immediate moment of feeling and assist the process rather than be compliant with children's demands.

- When working with parents we can model deferring needs for clients and then better equip them through modelling, for them to show children that they have heard and appreciated their emotional state and mirrored that back to them. They then feel valued, heard and have a model of how to deal with emotions.

- Employ the above suggestions on getting adult needs met elsewhere and children's needs met unconditionally by adults. Also review the notion of being an unconditional 'giver'. Believe this.

- Create divisions between work and relating. This is especially hard if work or study is being performed at home.

- Get help from a counsellor or therapist on being emotionally present.

- Check that the parent client has an emotional vocabulary to talk with. Check that they can join emotional words with people's face states and body expression.

In summary: parents need to put their own emotions aside and to listen.

Lack of empathy

Some parents have so much stress or distress that they withdraw empathy from their children. This is common in couple break-ups when the adults are so involved in their own distress that they can say something like, 'The kids seem to be handling it just fine.' It is likely that it will look like that to them due to their withdrawal of empathy to focus on themselves. Children without empathy are children who are lonely, as they have lost a needed part of life: unconditional love. They have a right to feel angry about that.

Giving assistance

Reduction of that stress is important:

- Generate a culture of being able to think all the time what children are thinking and feeling and check out your assumptions with other adults and the child. What is it like to be in young skin?

- That means that we don't just relate to our own childhood but understand the things of our children's childhood too. We need to know typical things that are part of early childhood life. Can we sense the hurt behind the bravado of a loud aggressive boy, feel the abandonment of having everyone fuss over a child's new baby brother?

- We need to understand children's dependence on adults for their needs, that they feel frightened and insecure when they hear Mum and Dad fight.

- If a parent has Asperger syndrome or is on the autism spectrum, provide the parent with the means to access support and advice if needed.

- Reduce parental stress by ensuring core needs such as food, warmth, clothes, and safety and security are met.

- Assist the adult to ask questions and listen to answers that are about the child and the child's feelings.

- Adults, when tuned to the needs of children, are often motivated to act and free themselves from feeling hopelessness.

In summary: reduce the focus on the adult's needs and shift it to the child's. View the world from the child's eyes.

Selfishness, blaming and resentment

With the delay in parenting by the current generation of new parents, many are not having their first child until the age of 32. This follows possibly 15 years of living independently, being well paid, enjoying a good lifestyle and travelling.

For many the first child is a shock and an abrupt change of lifestyle and self-gratification that was not experienced to the same extent by their parents. Some resent the reduced freedom and others refuse to accept the change and try to cling to past lifestyles.

New parents experience a transition in values, income and relationships. It is important to pass through that transition and move to a new reality for the wellbeing of the couple and the new child. This adjustment can be helped by accepting that as parents they now must be prepared to give and give, and love doing that. I recall an indigenous elder saying at a meeting, 'If you don't have time for your kids, don't have them', and another poster which claimed 'Kids are not a new accessory. They are the centre of the universe.'

Giving assistance

For many struggling new parents it helps if some old ideas and values can be abandoned and new relationship-oriented ones taken on. Some practical discussions can be quite challenging. Professional helpers may find the following helpful to say:

> 'Children take over your life. If you have them, then give in and make them number one. They will pay back ten-fold.'

> 'You will want your children at your bedside when you die, not your party mates.'

> 'Children will want love, attention and appreciation, much more than a new car; but they can't tell you that because they're children.'

Talk of parental teams so that parents understand that they should work and support each other and act together.

Talk to fathers in terms of challenges: 'Are you up to it?'; 'Do you think that you are in control of your own temper?'; 'What example do the children see?'

In summary: *give in and give*. Children are worth it.

Feeling powerless

All parents come to parenting incomplete. At some stage parents will feel useless, hurt, fearful and maybe even sad. Some parents did not have adequate parental care and modelling. Some were born in turmoil, some had disabled or unwell parents, not to mention parents who misused alcohol, and some experienced family violence. Knowing that we are all in some way incomplete can assist parents, although some parents will be dealing with more struggles than others. Good therapy and counselling can assist in replacing missing elements, loosen jammed emotional processes such as grief, help the parent to forgive and let go of the past, generate adult perspectives and develop coping skills. If the sense of powerlessness is expressed through anger, then there is good potential for modelling constructive action, but if it is continually expressed in a manner that displaces blame and retribution from the past onto the new generation, then intergenerational abuse is perpetuated.

Giving assistance

- Assist them in following the model of the 'anger flow' diagram on p.84.

- Clear assessment of things in the past can lead to clear decisions by the caregiver to act, either for or against her children, in parenting: 'I made a decision that I would never hit my kids.'; 'I made a decision that I would give my kids all the support at school that they need, not like what happened to me.'

- Recognize and deal with problems as they come up. Deal with old hurts, let go of old losses, forgive, strategize to not let bad things happen. Get professional help and support when you need it.

Treating children like adults

Children have the brains, bodies and knowledge of children and it is essential to their development that they have a chance to grow fully and fairly to the best of their potential. Failure to provide that environment damages neural, physical, relational, emotional and cognitive growth (Bartley 2006; Eriksen 1963). Children are children and are entitled to the freedom and childishness of being a child. Being able to lie with full trust in protecting and loving arms is essential to developing a positive and relational approach to life.

We can abuse this is by making children do duties beyond their age or treating them like adults in relationships. Sometimes, due to the lack of adult support and encouragement for the parent, the parent may push a child into a parenting role. It is not a fair choice to make a child fulfil that role. Such negative actions could mean making the child 'My little man' or even a substitute for a partner, or making a girl do the housework. It could be expecting a child to understand adult concepts and words or not to enjoy childish language.

Many adults seek therapy for 'lost childhoods' where they were expected to do the work, relating and responsibility of an adult. Older children are more prone to this, as are single-parented children and children with parents who are disabled or have an addiction (Jurkovic 1997).

Giving assistance

- Point the behaviour out to the parent and make them aware of the rights of the child to their childhood.

- Generate adult support for the parent/s.

- Organize some freedom for the child so that she is able to have some 'child time'.

- Invite the child to do 'free child' things like dancing under the hose and being naughty, lighting a fire, pillow fights and so on.

In summary: let children enjoy their childishness and don't use them to make up for your own needs.

Crisis management – forgetting the child

We all have crises but some people don't act to stop them happening or let them happen again and again. While caregivers are having a crisis, their children experience that crisis through them. Additionally, if caregivers put all their energy into the crisis, there may be no one helping the child manage the anxiety and to change it. Break-ups are the worst example of this.

Giving assistance

- Take the client through reflective learning cycles to prevent recycles and cautions for the future.

- Get good support for children if the parents are not coping. Have a child advocate in action to give a voice to young ones who cannot talk to the distress but show it through their actions.

- Generate empathy by using empathic questions.

In summary: *act to solve things quickly*. Call others to help. Don't just do it by yourself. Notice the effect on the children and help them.

Disrespect and devaluing

If there is any form of disrespect in the home, to any member of the family, then it will affect any child in that home. It is impossible for it not to. Children sense conflict, tension and negativity through language, physical expression and non-verbal cues (Frodl *et al.* 2010). Constant bossing around, put-downs, name-calling, manipulating, criticism, neglect, control and stress taint the whole home atmosphere and, in severe forms, it can damage a child's neural development.

Giving assistance

- Use good screening questions to encourage confidential disclosures.
- Check support systems that are in place or need to be in place.
- Develop a plan for exit and security elsewhere, should this be necessary.
- Educate as to the harm of action and atmosphere.
- Help establish a 'verbal negativity is not okay' rule for the home.

In summary: stop devaluing and disrespect. Generate consequences and boundaries.

Dominating parent

Witnessing a parent being a lesser or secondary parent has an effect on both the gender models and on the model of what a relationship looks like. The repetition of the same pattern for either gender is part of intergenerational patterns of relation and often dysfunctional family dynamics. Equality and respect need to be modelled by both parents as modern ways of relating. It one parent is being talked down to, bossed around or fearful of the other, then it teaches the child disrespect, and this may well be reproduced in the next generation. Common ways for fathers to act unequally are shouting or being physically threatening, autocratic and punitive. Common ways for mothers to act unequally are ordering other adults around, making all the decisions about parenting, socializing and household décor, and attempting to control children's perspectives about the other parent.

Children generally have a strong wish to love and be loved by both parents, equally. Observing devaluing behaviour confuses their perspective on the worth of that parent, or worse, it generates sides and a wish by the child to rescue one parent from the other. Both parents may be dominating and controlling in different spheres. Children often feel torn between such parents and stressed within the dynamics.

Giving assistance

- Educate as to the effects of children witnessing unequal or disrespectful relating.

- Urge the 'busy' party to divulge and trust the other to do some of the work. Examine the benefits of sharing more equally, which usually means less stress and more free time.

- Use the words 'old fashioned' and 'modern' to describe the contrasting patterns and ask which they want to be.

In summary: *parents need to address each other as equals and respect each other's opinions and rights.* The best ways to teach children how to have caring, equal and respectful relationships is to demonstrate them.

Conflict resolution for parents

Children learn more from their parents or primary caregivers than from anyone else. The dependency and the real-life nature of the relating make parents the greatest influence in a child's life. The model that we display of dealing with conflict is the one that they are most likely to copy. So, if we don't like a child's behaviour, the first question is, 'Do I do that too?'

Helping practitioners may ask a parent sensitively, 'What do you model in dealing with conflict? Do you frighten people? Do you manipulate people? Do you talk down or over others? Do you threaten? Do you do "dramas" and "performances"? Are you stubborn, do you not listen, lack understanding, fail to consider, or sneak and outwit or guilt-trip others?'

Conflict is an essential part of life. For most, it is unpleasant, but expressing it out loud is part of having an open and clear relationship. Conflict allows change and everything has to change at some point. Creative conflict allows the release of anger feelings in a manner that is respectful, expressive and motivates problem solving.

Giving assistance

Parents and caregivers in institutions may find the following useful:

- Decide what your need is, or what you want to happen or to change.

- Practise words for it that won't inflame the situation.

- Say out loud what it is to the person who needs to hear.

- Say it in a way or tone or at a time that will allow the person to hear it.

- If they haven't got the message, then you haven't communicated it very well.

- Try to give reasons.

- Ask them to tell you what they think they have heard you say.
- Listen to the other perspective. Repeat back what you have heard about their viewpoint.
- Hear emotions that are lying behind your differences, especially fear.
- Talk about vulnerable emotions.
- Look for a common need.
- Look for a way of having both your needs met so that you can both win.
- Acknowledge small things to agree on, then try to build to bigger things.
- Don't give in just to keep the peace.
- Never abuse the other person.
- Create an atmosphere where you can have a friend at the end of the argument.
- Keep talking, talking, talking.
- Take time out for a break if you think things are getting stuck, or too charged.
- Take time out if you need to have a think about it.
- When you think you have an agreement, summarize it completely to make sure you both have heard the same thing and that you both agree.
- Be prepared to try something for a short time and review it at the end.
- If there is little resolution and it is hard work, have the discussion in front of a third person.
- If there is likely to be stronger anger, many people are more restrained if they meet in a public place, such as a cafe.
- Thank the other person when they seem to understand you.
- Thank the other person when they make a concession.
- Thank the other person for completing the conflict successfully.
- Thank yourself for looking after your position and your needs.

In summary: never do or say anything that you wouldn't want your child to copy.

Practitioners may find the following a sensitizer for a useful conversation with a parent or caregiver.

CHECKLIST FOR RAISING HAPPY CHILDREN

Are you providing these for your child:

- a chance to explore within safe boundaries
- opportunities for emotional expression within safe boundaries
- reflection of the child's feelings
- affection, including hugs and cuddles
- time together
- time for each child
- exercise and physical activity
- playtime with your child and playtime for your child alone
- rest and quiet times
- soothing experiences (singing, music, blowing bubbles, rocking, holding)
- reading to your child
- giving your child an emotional language (see p.47 and pp.72–74)
- sharing new experiences and talking about them
- explaining to a child why she needs to do 'this' or not do 'that'
- limits set in a clear, firm, consistent and positive way
- helping children to see the consequences of their behaviour
- showing your child a loving adult relationship
- modelling good communication
- modelling good time out
- telling family stories that are positive and fun
- telling jokes and fooling around
- turning the television off to talk
- helping a child to order and structure her environment (put away toys, have places for things, have routines, put things in order of size, group objects in a child's environment such as 'shoes go here, t-shirts go here')
- an opportunity for expression of anger (a pillow to punch, newspaper to tear up, crayons and paper for scribbling, boots to stomp in)

- good listening to anger and child fury
- shared family meal times
- shared play experiences that teach boundaries and taking turns
- age-appropriate toys, games and play
- adventure play for under-fives
- giving an opportunity for creative play (painting, modelling, play dough, building) and pretend play
- noticing and affirming a child's achievements, no matter how small they may seem
- saying 'Yes' more than 'No'
- sharing joyful experiences and reflecting a child's excitement, pride and happiness
- expanding the family unit to include family and friends who can share family fun and support the family
- including grandparents
- ensuring that those who have contact with a child are safe to be with (that they are not sexually, emotionally or physically abusive)
- helping a child to feel loved and secure and have a sense of belonging within the family and later to the wider community and culture.

Hitting and abuse

Several countries have completely banned the hitting of children. There are many more that, without banning hitting, have greatly restricted physical discipline. All cultures, to different degrees, put great value on children as precious and the foundation of the future. This seems to be in contradiction to laws that allow hitting. We reconcile this disparity somewhat by considering that the smacking of children is seen to be 'for the child's good' or that it is done with good intention and may even express the parent's caring concern.

There are some things that are of concern about this. First, physical correction is usually associated with the parent's anger rather than being delivered as a calm and calculated correction. Second, it is designed to hurt rather than enskill or develop understanding and reason. The act is associated with anger and is reactive through physical power. Is this the best way to train a child in the world, and what is the long-term outcome of this practice?

We suggest the policy of not hitting or smacking for the following reasons:

- Hitting teaches children that this is the way to solve problems. Connecting anger with physical coercion may lead to the breaking of laws of assault as adults, with far more damage done due to sheer adult size.

- Through learning via this method of 'fixing things' the child may learn no other options. The ability to resolve conflict through language is the most prevalent and socially sanctioned form of conflict resolution.

- Hitting and smacking hurts not just physically but emotionally, psychologically and spiritually. Certainly harsh words can act in a similar way so there also needs to be recognition of the power of language.

- Children will store resentment for a period of time which may be anywhere from a few minutes to a few decades. The anger, resentment, hurt, powerlessness, shame and feeling of being bullied for years will get in the way of later adult relationships.

- The resentment may be carried and the child may hit the hitter back when they are old enough. When this happens the carer has no other resources to execute in order to maintain the boundaries that an adolescent invariably still needs. The adolescent may then enter a period of boundarylessness and retributional shaming of the parent who may complain, 'I just can't control him/her.'

- Hitting manages behaviour through hurt and fear. It works. However, it only works for as long as the child is small or able to be dominated. It is short term and there is always a point at which it will not work. It is better, early on, to decide to have other ways to guide and boundary a child's behaviour. A system built on respect and empathy works for a far longer time – in fact, usually for life.

What arguments can be used by a professional against hitting (or 'smacking') children?

- Ask: 'Assuming that you will one day stop hitting your child, the question arises "What will you do then?"' Or, 'One day your child will be too big to smack, so what will you do then?'

    Response: A shrug or 'Then I'll do it by talking.'

    Reply: 'Why don't you do that now?'

- 'What comes to your mind first about your parent's discipline?' The answer from a hitting parent is usually an incident when they 'got the belt' or 'a good hiding'.

    The next question is: 'How was that? Did you like it?'

    Answer: 'Maybe not, but I deserved it', or 'Didn't do me any harm.'

Reply: 'Well, it justified hitting your own kids. How come it was the first thing that you remembered about discipline? How about leaving your kids a pleasant memory of your guidance?'

- Ask: 'If your kids were here now what would they say? Would they be too scared to tell the truth?'
- 'Do you like hurting them?'
- 'Isn't it more about you being physical because you are angry, rather than good discipline? Do your kids watch out for you when you are angry?'
- 'If you had another way to correct them that didn't involve hitting and that really worked, would you be interested?'

Dealing with rationalizations, minimizing and blaming

'I just smack'

Smacking is just another form of hitting. We have worked with too many parents who, due to rage, then guilt after smacking, have called hitting 'just smacking' so that they are able to feel better about it. Smacking is hitting, and it hurts, which is why it is done, so we need to find a more positive way of getting things done so that we don't damage our child and damage our relationship with the child. Would the parent or caregiver want their child to be doing that back to them in 20 years' time?

'It hurts me more than it does them'

The hurt that people say they feel doing physical correction is more a genuine hurt of themselves in the form of guilt and shame at what they are doing. It is that instant after the hit that they feel bad and then say, rightly, that the hurt is the bad feeling concerning what they have just released in a hitting form. Then they have to deal with that feeling by acting as if they are the martyr.

'It's for their own good'

After feeling disappointment and guilt, rationalization kicks in to take away the discomfort. Parents or caregivers rationalize that it is '*for their* [the child's] *own good*'. The 'good' they mean is that it may stop the child doing something that they shouldn't do, but they know that in the long run it is not for their own good as discussed above. They know other ways are better.

'God/the Bible/the church says that I should spare the rod and spoil the child'

The above quote, 'Spare the rod and spoil the child' does not appear in the Bible. It is a proverb that is not meant to be taken literally, and it means that if you fail to discipline your child, then this will disadvantage them. This is true. Children who have not been boundaried and given structure, protocols and successful ways of behaving are severely disadvantaged when it comes to getting on with people. But it does not mean hitting your children. Sometimes other verses are misinterpreted from scriptures of all faiths. Most philosophies and faiths suggest that children are precious and are to be guided with love and care.

Working with parents on smacking

When working with parents who have hitting problems we have often asked what the difference is between a hit and a smack. There are two interesting facts that come out of this work:

- *A large group are never able to clearly define a difference.* Parents sent to programmes for anger management and parenting describe smacking as being done both with hands and instruments (such as a stick, spoon or belt, fist or hand). They do not agree as to what is okay and what is not okay as a smack. They are unable to agree as to how hard is *too* hard. Some say when it makes a mark, some say when the child cries, and some say when it hurts you more. All of these sound a bit too late.

- *When the parent sees the effect/mark, they rationalize/minimize to deal with the guilt* of the hurt to someone that they invariably really love. Shame prevents open honesty so they minimize and make it less than it was. Comments such as 'It didn't hurt'; 'They made me do it'; 'It was just a smack' may even be followed by actions of covering the hand mark up so others can't see. The guilt and shame are rationalized, minimized and blamed on the child as a way of the hitter feeling better.

- *There is so much focus on the pain and surviving the pain, children forget what it was for.* Although the child has been hit, the intensity of the pain in that moment drives all consciousness into survival rather than guiding the consciousness into listening and accepting the real reasons why it was not a good idea to do it. All that they will remember is the punishment as a deterrent.

Ask an older person about getting the strap or cane at school. They will remember the hitting happening, but can they clearly tell you what it was for? This is obviously not always true as sometimes it does work and a child may say, 'No I won't do that or go there, as I will get hit.' In these cases notice that the rational reason is not because 'my parent loves me and wants me to stay safe from the danger of a situation' or that it's unkind to embarrass a parent in front of their friends. They just remember that 'you don't do it because you get hit', not the real reasons why it is unwise to do it. When limits are set by way of punishment, children do not learn to transfer the real reasons to another situation. For instance, a child who is smacked for jumping on the sofa will assume the strictures apply to that sofa then and there and go on to jump on some other sofa or chair or bed. Instead, children learn that it is advisable to do bad things in secret where they won't be found out and punished. Punishing children in this way does not teach them what they have done wrong and why the behaviour was wrong. It is from understanding why we should not do something that we begin to develop respect for others and their property, and out of that comes self-discipline.

Helena was walking home with her small daughter one day when her daughter ran ahead and straight across a main road. Helena was upset because a car was coming and only just stopped in time. Helena smacked her daughter hoping that she would learn not to do it again. Several times after they got home Helena asked, 'Why did Mummy smack you?' The only reply her daughter would give was 'You hit me!' Even a few days later the little girl had no idea why she had been smacked. Mum's anger was about the possible loss of her daughter. She had ended up converting this into pain for her daughter.

Hitting leaves a deeper mark than the skin

It is easy to feel that it has all gone away and can be forgotten when the mark of a hit goes. It hasn't. The act damages the mental wellbeing and the spirit of the child. There is psychological and spiritual damage. The younger the age when these things happen, the more damage they end up doing.

What goes round comes round, or the rule of karmic forces

Everything that we do to hurt or damage children, either on purpose or by accident, will come back on us at some point. We may wonder why we are having so much trouble now and we may wonder why our adolescent is being so difficult (when others seem to have quite co-operative and respectful children) and the answer lies in the memory and storage of hurt and injustice that are revisited when a child has increased power to express and repay. Payback may also be to uninvolved or innocent parties, such as educators.

Children who are routinely smacked are more likely to hit out at others when they are cross or frustrated. Some say that smacking teaches a child respect. It is more likely that children learn to fear. Respect requires us to value and understand another person, not fear them. Parents will often face a dilemma when faced with a defiant child: to follow the downloaded hitting imprint in their own software and do what was done to them, or think through a course of action that will help a child to learn a better way of behaving.

Foster a world based on increased respect rather than passing on bad things that have happened to us.

Damage to children

There are other ways that we can damage our children. These involve:

- deliberate action – for example, hitting is an action involving chosen behaviour

- accidental action – for example, forgetting to pick a child up from playcentre

- unconscious action – this involves not being aware that something was harming a child – for example, not realizing that a baby needs constant physical contact. Parents also need to be aware of different categories of damaging behaviour.

What is damaging behaviour and abuse?

Abuse leaves a child angry. Reducing abuse reduces anger in the present and the future. Parents often have quite extreme notions of what abuse is and fail to realize that smaller acts are also harmful and, when repeated, can have an accumulative effect. A child has a right to grow up without abuse, neglect or disrespect.

VERBAL ABUSE AND DISRESPECT

Putdowns	Promising and not delivering
Name-calling	Criticism
Shouting	Shouting
Lies	Labelling
Sarcasm	Threats

SEXUAL

Bad touching with hands or object

Bad sex talk/words

Showing sexual pictures

Seeing inappropriate acts

Oral, anal or vaginal intrusion

Creating sexual secrets

Shaming sexual organs

SPIRITUAL

Any type of abuse reduces the spirit

Not loving

Guilt making

Hating

Fear making

Acting oppressively and reducing joy

Making child feel bad or unworthy

PROPERTY

Stealing

Taking/hiding things away

Withholding

Disregard for a child's attachment to an object

Breaking/damaging

PHYSICAL

Shaking

Dropping

Pushing

Jabbing

Kicking

Locking up

Leaving in danger

Tying clothes too tight

Slapping

Smothering

Biting

Not keeping the child warm

EMOTIONAL OR MENTAL

All other forms of abuse	Being chaotic
Rejecting	Being harsh
Shaming	Abandoning
Creating insecurity	Over-controlling
Making fun	Leaving unattended
Withholding love	Ignoring
Neglect	Not holding, not cuddling
Being inconsistent	Manipulation
Taunting and teasing	Bad mouthing another parent

Professionals are ethically bound to stop all abuse, disrespect and negligence whenever they are aware of it. In many places this may involve mandatory reporting to authorities. Protecting parents, or continuing to believe that the professional can solve the problem, or the belief that if the parent is supported then the child is also supported, has resulted in some horrific historic cases. Often, dramatic change is needed to create a shift, and bringing the private into the public sphere can be that stimulus.

The law does not cover subtler forms of abuse, however. It is still the professional's moral and ethical duty to act to stop or reduce parents' or caregivers' behaviour that damages children. This may even require the professional to ask whether their practice is free of neglect or disrespect and whether all the child's needs are being met, because failure to meet needs, not just of warmth and safety but also of love and affirmation, is a form of neglect. Fear of losing a client may draw a professional into collusion. Professional supervisors and professional membership organisations are great sources of advice and generators of ethical reflection. They are there to refine thinking in those moments of professional loneliness.

Children need many parents

The reduction of fear, hurt, shame, insecurity and loss means that there is less reason for anyone feeling angry, particularly a child.

While this is a chapter on parents and parenting, it is worth acknowledging the fluidity of the term 'parent' and how diverse family models can be. Single parents may feel stretched, two parents may feel trapped, but for thousands of years children have grown up with multiple parental figures.

The nuclear family was an invention of the industrial revolution when families were brought into city living and separated into rooms where children lived only with a mother and father. These rooms became the suburbs. Before this time we all lived in villages where our families had lived for generations and every child had uncles, aunts, grandparents and great-grandparents living nearby, if not in the same house. Children had many parents who all looked out for them. Later, as parents struggled with the difficulty of bringing children up in the new nuclear family, even these units broke up and many households had only one person raising children. Many so-called developing countries are undergoing this transition to a nuclear family now as they become more industrialized. China, India and African countries are good examples. Along with the shift to the nuclear family is an increase in many social problems and increased individualism that risks the most dangerous disease of all – isolation. Isolation is at the heart of mental illness, suicide, depression, and a contributing influence in child abuse, family violence, youth violence and drug and alcohol problems (Ilardi 2009).

The isolation of a child

Imagine being a child with a single parent and that parent gets angry with you. Suddenly the only person in the world who cares about you, and whom you are dependent on, doesn't love you, or so it seems. Imagine being a child hearing two parents fighting, as they all will do at some point. Suddenly the young child is afraid that she may lose one or both parents or worse, get caught in taking sides in the fighting. What the child needs is a third parent who can say, 'Hey, don't worry, I am here to look after you and they are only fighting.' ('It will pass and you are secure.')

Has the family you are working with got three 'parents'? They can be grandparents, godparents, neighbours, close, long-term family friends – as long as they are regularly there and available. A measure may be, could they be asked to a family meeting? Bringing nuclear families together in the same street or housing block allows for a partial presence if doors are open and children can walk. As soon as dependence on vehicles for transport enters the equation, there is a shift to independence not interdependence. Getting to parts of the extended family need to be pedestrian, short and safe.

The extended family unit has a considerable advantage:

- It allows for a child and any participant to be exposed to many ideas, ways of doing things (from cooking to changing tyres, from religion to enterprise) and presents them to the child for the child to choose or be attracted to.

- It prevents and dissolves the power of a sole parent's influence over a child, through that child's dependence on the parent in the child's formative stages. Having just one or two parents leaves a child open to believing the ideas and fears of just one adult (from the belief that the other parent is a bad person to the right to steal, devalue education, or through to the idea that the child is bad). Having 'many parents' prevents intense involvement with one perspective.

- It allows a large enough group to moderate bad behaviour and the effect that behaviour has on a child, adult or group. Other adults can moderate the behaviour of one adult and bring it into context. For a child, having comparisons and options of models reduces the power and influence of one model if it is bad.

- It is a larger economic unit with many support sources that can manage variations of fortune and crisis. When good or bad things happen the effect is flattened as it is absorbed and cushioned by numbers. The loss of an income can be sustained by others supporting the collective and the minor parts during times of hardship. Individual incomes are of less consequence.

- In globalized times, when there is an increase in competition for resources and great inequality, sharing is an important value and possibly the answer to survival.

- It allows parents to better respond to engagements and forces external to the family, due to the possibility of instant childcare. Such forces may be jobs, adventures and opportunities, education, or protection and security.

- It allows a temporary shift of parenting from a set of parents to a secondary set of parents without the trauma of abandonment and of new affiliation and trust building.

- It makes for a more public life of its family members and increases the accountability of the family members to each other. More public living reduces the possibility of secrecy of perversion and abuse. Arguments are monitored and support given before reducing to severe abuse. The possibility of non-condoned behaviour is less likely and can be made more accountable through the more visible nature of the family actions and relationships – in a nuclear family sexual secrets are more easily held when there is only one other adult who may be frequently absent.

- It generates the possibility of challenge by members to support compliance to social norms. Accountability to norms of full participation and respect is created.

- It reduces some of the shame of a family as it deals with an individual's dysfunction and presents large group approval. Deeds and conditions that may be shameful can be countered through large group support. Having a child with a disability or a mental illness in the family is a manageable condition and is less shameful if the child is loved and protected by inclusion into a larger group.

- It exposes the child to diversity due to numbers involved. Large families may contain diverse occupations, ages, gender options, sexuality, hopes and characters.

- Most importantly of all, it reduces the loneliness of its members at a time when we know that isolation is the major key to generating crime, ill health, low esteem and hopelessness. Relationships bring inspiration, co-operation, achievement, and health and wellbeing.

Having stated the above it does need to be recognized that the extended family is not perfect and can suffer dysfunction too. Extended families need to watch for non-benevolent power cliques and hierarchy, closed groups, class-bound identities, and support for outdated values such as sexism.

There are also extraordinary cases where a lone parent has overcome all of these disadvantages and managed to beat the odds. Remarkable examples do not, however, prove the case for promoting single adult parenting and nor do they disprove the norm of high levels of social problems from under-parented family units. These comments are not intended in any way to devalue the remarkable hard work and effort of single and nuclear families, however. The evidence suggests that the task requires more than one adult and that single parents are therefore likely to be the hardest working parents of all. We ask, is that necessary or even fair?

The nuclear family is, of course, not always isolated from the other parts of the family, and we suggest that linking the parts and sharing responsibility within a wider circle is a professional practice that will improve the wellbeing of the family, children and their future chances. An approach, then, is to generate a pseudo-extended family through increasing occasional and distant contact and inclusion of extended family in children's welfare meetings.

The African proverb 'It takes a village to raise a child' is true of all cultures. In times past, the people of our villages used to have the authority to manage and befriend all the children of the village, and there were many parents sharing the load and giving security and guardianship. We suggest that one- and two-parent nuclear families are really a stressful and insufficient way of bringing up children.

We believe that the nuclear family is a somewhat failed experiment and that the future of the planet depends on larger family units to support children and prevent increased isolation, individuation, independence, the self-gratification of consumerism, dependence on an anonymous state instead of relationships, and that better wellbeing is achieved by larger units of care and protection. We can expect children to more often feel angrier if they are left with strangers, and to be less secure as parents go into conflict and separate.

Professional helpers should find some more 'parents' for the children they work with. Fear, hurt and insecurity are the basis of most anger in children. Constant parenting and a place of belonging help take this away.

Professional practice needs to increase and foster links with other linked parts of a family, use placement with extended families rather than foster care, increased conflict and mediation services to prevent units fragmenting and therapy for dysfunctional parts so that they can better parent children.

TEACH A PUPPY WHEN IT IS YOUNG

Children under the age of five are wonderfully flexible and open to learning. As each year passes the patterns of thinking and behaving become more established and neural pathways more established. Now is the best time to be the best influence we can. Poor influence now may take much longer later to undo and establish differently.

Parents are in an extraordinary position in the first five years to be a huge influence over who their child will be.

DO IT RIGHT NOW

It is easier to change a little child. It lasts longer. It goes deeper. It makes the rest of your parenting easier and less work. It makes the rest of your child's life easier and less work.

It makes adolescence a breeze rather than a reactive struggle.

Professionals have the hugely worthwhile occupation of helping make the world a better place to be in. They have the chance to support parents to have the opportunity to create wonderful children. As both parents and professionals, we are aware, however, that there are no perfect parents, and that parents grow into the role and learn a lot about life, relationships, personal issues and responsibility as they go. The questions below may be thoughtful sensitizers to provoke choice and action.

ARE YOU THE GROWN-UP? A CHECKLIST FOR WORKING WITH PARENTS

What we bring from our past has a big influence on the way we parent and so the happiness or upset of our children. Here is a checklist of some of the things that we need to have attended to if we are going to do the best for our children and model adult action.

	No	Yes
Are you able to…		
stop and think when you feel angry?		
model time out when you are angry or stressed?		
notice the signs of anger in your body?		
empathize and quickly imagine what it is like to be a small child?		
set boundaries and keep your word every time?		
keep promises?		
play with your children?		
tell your children that you love them?		
put your own feelings to one side to deal with your children first?		
control children in a way that doesn't kill adventure and spirit?		
set and maintain unpopular boundaries?		
handle your partner giving all his/her attention to the children?		
find time to spend with your children and put your children before work?		
not blame others, including your children?		
treat your children like children, not adults or friends?		
strategize to improve situations and do something about problems?		
ask for help?		
never put up with abuse?		
look for the positive in children, not just the negative?		
let go of the past and not hold grudges or resentment?		
sing in your home?		
laugh out loud and joke with your children?		
listen to anger?		
let go of old scores with all your previous partners?		
treat your children as future free spirits, not possessions?		
not use your children to punish a separated parent?		
create something positive out of accident and misfortune?		
plan your parenting style together?		
plan when you want to have children so that you are able to meet their needs?		

	No	Yes
Do you...		
read to your children?		
protect your children from harm?		
have other adults around you who tell you that you are worthwhile and okay?		
always have a caring adult with your child when you are absent?		
keep sober when you are with them?		
talk about the importance of school and learning for them?		
handle your children being angry with you and not liking you?		
handle your children feeling sad, angry, anxious, upset or disappointed without rescuing them?		
have the ability to be yourself, not pretending and acting in front of others?		
have the ability to be honest?		
know what you *wouldn't* do from your own childhood?		
know what your children need for their age?		
avoid ever abusing others – children or partner?		

	No	Yes
Have you...		
got a good, friendly relationship with your own mother?		
got a good, friendly relationship with your own father?		
healed from hurting from your own childhood?		

Most people will have a 'no' answer somewhere in this list. This is an opportunity to make some changes.

The following is a useful and thoughtful activity for parents that will provoke professional discussions.

Exercise: A plan for your support network

Parents all need help at some time in their family lives, particularly when they are parenting small children. For some parents it may be useful to check through with them on the following list.

Do they have:

- appropriate people and organisations they can turn to for help?

- someone who they can call when they are furious?

- someone who can look after their child when they need time out?

- someone who can take their child when the child needs time out from others (including the parent)?

- someone who can provide reliable medical advice if their child is sick?

- someone who can talk with their child when the parent can't?

- someone the parent can cry with?

- someone the child can cry with?

- someone who can advise the parent on parenting skills?

- someone who the parent can talk to when they are depressed?

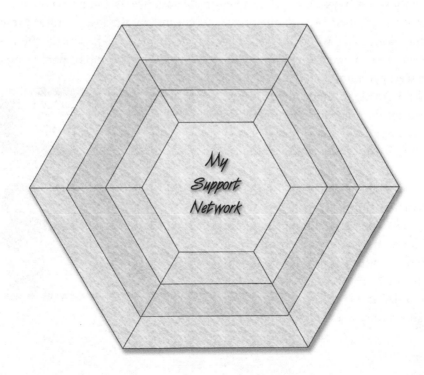

Chapter 10

Engaging with Fathers

Fathers and parenting

We include a chapter specifically dedicated to engaging with fathers here, given that this group of parents are often neglected, and yet can have a substantial impact on the behaviour of a child if they are engaged.

New parents have choices now that no other generation of parents have had in 300 years. Advisors and supporters need to know some things about fathers as they have to some extent been regarded as accessories in some circles, with damaging influences for children.

In the past, we would say that mothers have done too much parenting and men too little. Expectations of fathers actively parenting little children had reduced over the years to almost exclude fathers altogether. This disadvantaged everyone – the child, the father and most of all, the mother. Things have changed. Mothers will get more balance, wellbeing and enjoyment if they are able to include and trust fathers. It is important for the child to have experience of affirming men, and especially so for boys. Later in life, many male adolescents and grown men report anger at their fathers because they have felt cheated by the low nurturer presence of their father and what he *could* have given them if he had been there in a nurturing role for them. Questioning of stereotypical roles could be part of looking at stressed parenting.

Children highly dependent on just one parent find the world a more risky place to be in as there is only one person giving that trust, care and reassurance. So when the parent is unwell, stressed, angry with them or absent, the child has lost the only person in the world who loves them. Children therefore need a number of adults to bring them up. Fathers often do not feel confident about parenting, and may believe that the mother is the expert. They forget that she is only a few months ahead in

learning those skills herself at the time of pregnancy. The best things that mothers can do are:

- encourage the father to participate
- stand back to let the father in
- not criticize the father
- let the father do things differently
- go out and leave the father to it!

Professionals are in a situation of supporting fathers and having clear advantages in the form of more fathers involved in childcare and preschool education, in discussion on behavioural issues and generating unity in parenting changes. There is mounting evidence on the positive effects of fathers being involved in children's education and reading (Fatherhood Institute 2010; Goldman 2005). Fathers will take more responsibility if left alone with children for periods of time and respond to direct invitations to be involved in external organisations and activities. Mothers should be encouraged to take time out from babies and young children and to socialize, renew their energy or keep skilled for other tasks. The house may be a bit messy when the mother returns and the child's vest on back to front, but the occasion allows for relationship building and a claiming of fatherhood for the father. Fathers can clean up too, although they may do it differently.

Professional helpers should look out for the mother who feels the need to be in control all the time, and supervise the father in what to do and how to do it. This control is disempowering and destroys relationships, and is a stimulus for fathers avoiding opportunities in order to avoid maternal control. Care also needs to be taken to avoid making fathers the final port of call for discipline. Nurture and discipline are often stronger if shared between both parents.

It is essential to know that the sex and gender differences spoken of here will be evidenced in nearly all things. A man and a woman may perform any task, but they will do it differently. Males are different and children need to experience that difference.

Assisting fathers to think about fathers

There are four steps to helping a man in his fathering:

- know that fathering is important and why that is so
- know that fathering is different from mothering
- know the skills of relating as a father
- know that the father must claim the relationship with the child independent of the mother.

Fathers are important

Given the absence of fathers from many men's lives, new fathers often are unsure of the importance of fathers. Assisting a father to understand his importance is the first step to his active participation. Professionals need to take time to let the father know that his power as a male role model is vital, that being around to do things the 'boy-way' is immensely affirming, and that direct confirmation and praise by a male is essential. Under-fathered boys have much higher rates of mental and physical health problems, low esteem, crime, lower educational achievement, personal child abuse, abuse of others, partner abuse, drug and alcohol abuse and suicide (Blankenhorn 1995; Plantin, Olukoya and Ny 2011; Pruett 2002; Pruett and Pruett 2009). Fathering is important and will greatly advantage the father's children if he actively takes part and does it well. A boy who is under-fathered is entitled to feel angry about that deprivation, and usually does. Children need fathers.

Fathering is different from mothering

Because of genetic and socialized differences everything a father does, he does differently from a mother. Even the way he holds a baby is different. The way he plays, the way he changes clothes, the way he feeds a child, the way he talks is different. Apart from the benefit of experiencing diversity of relationships it gives knowledge to both boys and girls about men and therefore about one-half of the population. A loving male caregiver is emotionally instructive to children of how to do that themselves as future adults. It is also affirming for boys.

Know the skills of relating as a father

Time is the first essential and taking on the role as provider has traditionally been the greatest excuse for not having time. That has changed and is no longer an 'exit' due to changed earning roles and men realizing that there is great joy in paternal interaction and that paid work is not so important – the clear prioritizing of the child relationship is seen as a direct purpose for earning money. The second greatest skill is empathy, and the process of putting oneself into the tiny shoes of a young child is one of the safest things one can do. The earlier this connection and bond take place, the greater the likelihood of their being deep and continuing. Bonds with the child in the womb indicate better involvement later for the father.

Claiming the relationship independent of the mother

Many fathers do *secondary* parenting. This is old-style and mother-centric. Fathers, at some point, need to realize that they have to claim both the relationship for themselves as an important personal connection, and claim responsibility for making it happen. Secondary parenting is evidenced in comments from mothers such as: 'Remember to pick up Bobby'; 'Can you read Carla a story now?'; 'You need to take the kids with you.' The management of the parenting comes from the mother, and she organizes the father into his role. The father should claim his role by initiating the interaction such as: 'I'm taking Marcus fishing with me today.' The deal was struck out of something that happened between Marcus and his father, it needed no intermediary and was stated as a fact and not a request for permission. The mother comment of, 'Don't get the children too excited' is countered by 'Children are supposed to get excited' from the father (we know from research that fathers are good at that type of play and that children often seek to elicit that play; see Clarke-Stewart 1978; Lamb 1976, 1977). The father has his analysis of the situation that he takes a stand for. Unfortunately, however, some men don't claim fatherhood until they split up from their partner, and have the children to themselves, and even then some fail at that transition. Fathers then claim their relationship with their children and are instrumental in the expression of that relationship.

Advice for fathers

Emotions

Fathers often get to do the anger in the family and may miss out on doing all the other emotions including fear, sadness, hurt or love. A full range of emotions makes us balanced and healthy. Fathers who get to express all these emotions also model to their sons how to be a full human being, with strong nurture and feeling.

Get involved

It takes at least two adults to bring up children and they miss out on a lot of fun, love and reward if they don't have both. There is a notion in counselling and therapy that by doing the actions that were missed out on as a child, any deficit will be replaced. Nurturing a child as if it is you who is the child is reparative and intra-psychically healing.

Shared control

Sometimes mothers, usually by default, may seem to want to control the parenting. Fathers should not be afraid to push in and claim the space and the right. Usually the mother will respect the father and appreciate the sharing, the responsibility and the man. They should talk and co-operate on tasks and the child's future. The father should insist on time with the children when the mother is not around.

Male-to-male affirmation

Showing sons that they can come and talk to a male when they have a problem or are hurt allows them to have strong male relationships, to share male vulnerability and also not to be dependent on women. This allows them to go into an adult relationship on equal terms with women, as males confident in their masculinity, and with something strong and different to offer to that relationship. Fathers are also important for daughters, however. It is from fathers that daughters learn how to relate to the men in their lives and the men in their future, intimate relationships and to expect and accept unconditional love and respect.

Fathers and children's anger

Fathers also have different ways of doing the same things that mothers do, and children are enriched by that difference. However, many fathers and mothers underrate the value of father behaviour.

Perhaps the key attribute of fathers of young children is that they have the potential to reassure children that men are sources of nurture, love and assistance and thus form a basis of relating to men for the child's life. For boys especially they break the dependence on the mother, strengthen male identity and increase men's reliance on each other rather than continuing the isolation that many men living in Western countries experience, that is the source of so much depression and suicide (Biddulph 1995; Ilardi 2009).

As many men probably had minimal attention from their own fathers, professionals may need to purposefully assist fathers to consider the skills of care and intimacy.

Fathers may need encouragement to:

- listen quietly and carefully, especially to children's feelings
- pick children up and cuddle them
- acknowledge cuts, grazes and hurts for the pain that they cause the child, and go to the doctor with the chid if needed. Ask parents, 'Who does the child go to when upset or hurt?'
- acknowledge boys in particular and let them know that they can trust a man
- ask them how they would like things fixed or how a thing can be put right
- listen to others' stories about your child and ask people to be honest with you.

There are a few don'ts, coulds and shoulds, however, that are worth being specific about:

- Don't teach children to hit back.
- Don't hit people on a child's behalf; don't hit children (see pp.169–174 on smacking).
- Early childhood teachers and caregivers need to work with fathers if they have a problem, not just blame them or avoid them.
- Fathers teach many things when they wrestle with boys, such as maintaining regular, loving, physical contact.
- Don't rescue a child all the time; find out what is really going on.
- Fathers can do active things with the children and tire them out.
- Give permission for fathers to excite children.
- Fathers should get involved with babies as early bonding creates enduring relationships.
- Share childcare with mothers.
- Fathers should pick up babies if they are crying and carry them.
- Fathers should sing to children, especially at bed time.
- Fathers should tell stories to their child and have jokes with their child.
- Fathers should take their child to where other fathers go.
- Fathers should show children what they look like when they are angry and model good anger management, time out and conflict resolution.
- Fathers are usually firm on boundaries and rules; they should have consistent consequences.
- Fathers should include the child when doing things and let them copy behaviour and tasks, even though they may make a mess.
- Fathers should protect children from harm and advocate for them.
- Fathers should give compliments and positive feedback and love.

Fathers and sons wrestling

Somehow fathers and boys like to have fun, fight and wrestle. Mothers don't always know what to do about this as it can seem out of control and loud, and there may be fear that someone will be hurt. The best thing for mothers to do is leave the room. If it is right on bed time they can come back when it has all died down, and we suggest that the father can then calm the children down by reading a story. (Reading to boys in particular is a powerful model and research shows this is key in helping with boys' literacy (Goldman 2005).)

Boys and fathers wrestling is important. A lot of contact, communication and learning takes place when they wrestle. Some of the benefits are:

- *Learning rule and boundary setting*: The key rule is 'Nobody gets hurt.' Boys need to know that they have strength and this can be dangerous if they don't manage their bodies and strength. The idea is that boys can experiment with their physical power and the father can show the power that he has.

- *Learning empathy*: Empathy in this context is understanding that you can hurt somebody else and not doing that because you can imagine what it is like and you don't want that to happen. Neither the father nor the son wants to hurt someone that they love.

- *Power–energy exchange*: This is a boy thing, full of boy energy. When two males do this there is an energy exchange that creates bonding and connection. Women and girls are likely to do this by talking. Boys are likely to do it physically. The energy that passes between a father and son in wrestling builds this relationship.

- *Physical contact and intimacy*: The energy exchange goes further to create a sense of intimacy. There is nothing closer than feeling the breath of someone you like or love on your neck as they struggle in your embrace. This creates an intimacy that is hard to explain, but is full of love for both. This is often how a boy knows his father loves him – to wrestle body to body and not get hurt. Additionally it means the boy is not frightened of being close to males and can share comfortably with them. It prevents homophobia in that it makes good male contact healthy instead of fearful and makes strong contact without sexual connotations.

- *Power hierarchy*: Males like to know what the order of power and strength is. When that is clear they relax and work well together. Wrestling lets the boy know that the father is in charge and is stronger. This is reassuring and gives a feeling of safety and security. When the son can beat the father, the son will likely stop fighting and seek affirmation from other men.

- *Security*: There is great security for a boy in knowing that his father is strong and that he will use that strength to protect him. Then the boy can relax and be a boy. When there is no father around, a boy has the horrible responsibility of feeling that he has to protect his mother, no matter how old he is. This elevates the child in responsibility and emotional duty. Ideally the boy needs a childhood where he is able to feel that someone else is doing the protection and he can relax. Boys who see the father hurt the mother live in a terrible dilemma. It is then that they actually do want to beat the father in a fight. Up until then, they only wanted to know that the father could beat and protect them. Carried resentment and confused models result.

- *Physical/emotional release:* Wrestling is very physical and males release emotions through physical rather than verbal processes. Most stress, anxiety and tension can be released through a fortnightly wrestle, perhaps. If the relationship is good there is a cleanness and new liveliness alongside a peace and satisfaction in a boy who has just wrestled with his father.

Wrestling releases tension and anger and is an important part of a boy's life.

Anger at fathers

Anger at fathers is a major issue that is often brought into the counselling room by children and adults alike. A father's 'sins' may include:

- not being at the key event of a child's recognition (the sports cup etc.)
- being hard and at times abusive
- being over-controlling
- being drunk or under the influence of drugs
- hurting the mother
- being a 'broken' man
- accepting scorn or verbal abuse from the mother
- being unloving or showing little feeling
- being a friend instead of a parent
- and, worst of all, not being there at all or for long periods of time.

It is important for fathers to be there and a lot is expected of them. Few fathers get full marks, but it is really important for practitioners and educators to support and encourage contact and involvement. Many institutions are unaware of barriers and discrimination that have made it hard for fathers, especially those who do not live in the same house or who parent alone. Children want to love their fathers, not be angry with them. Fathers are usually prepared to die for their children, and are often highly motivated for change when confronted with the good of their children. Fathers are without doubt good for children (Pruett 2002).

Fathers, whether residential or distant, need to take responsibility for participation in the lives of their children. Some end up in secondary or passive parenting in that they allow themselves to be organized by the mother in their parenting action and relationships. Comments such as, 'Don't forget to come home in time for Jamie's birthday party' or 'How about reading Sasha a story?' or 'Can you pick Daniel up from swimming lessons?' suggest that the father is only doing his parenting through the mother's organization, not his own initiative. Children, especially boys, are often angry later on and report that they felt cheated out of their father's attention, affirmation and love through his distance, lack of initiative, own problems or lack of claiming his fatherhood role.

Early childhood educators should ensure the involvement of as many caring men as possible in the child's life, both on the basis of the child's need, the father's needs, the extended family structure and the increased participation of men in a caring community.

Chapter 11

Stories and Poems About Anger

Lucy's dress

Warwick Pudney and Josie Goulding

It was Monday morning. Monday was a playcentre day, the first after the weekend. Lucy was four and she loved playcentre. She could dig in the sand, climb the poles, pour water in the sink, make dough pies like Mum and cut pictures out of magazines. She was very good at cutting out pictures of dinners and cars, and never cut the heads off people.

'Hurry up Lucy and get dressed,' called Dad. Lucy pulled on her favourite dress with big red spots on it.

'You can't wear that dress,' called Mum. 'That's old and…'

'Why Mum? I like my dress…' said Lucy, disappointed.

'Well, it's not what the others are wearing dear. It's too, well…spotty.'

'I like my dress. I want to wear my dress,' said Lucy, looking like she might cry.

'Go and take it off Lucy,' ordered Mum.

'No, no, no. I want my red-spotted dress.'

'I said red spots were old. Just do it now…' Mum said, getting rather cross because she thought four-year-old girls were supposed to do what they were told.

Lucy stomped her feet and went back to her bedroom. She was very angry with Mum. It was her dress. And she liked her dress very much. Mum said the red spots were old. Well, she could fix that so Mum wouldn't say that she couldn't wear her dress.

She took the scissors from her play-drawer and sat down on the bed with her red-spotted dress all around her. One by one she stuck the scissors into the red spots and carefully cut them out. She was very good at cutting things out with her scissors. Soon she had cut all the big red spots out of her dress and had laid them on the bed around her. Maybe Mum would like her red-spotted bed, as long as she didn't take it to playcentre.

'Where are you, Lucy? Come on, we are late…oh great gobbling gooseballs, girl, what have you done?' gasped Mum. Lucy stood before her in a dress full of big neat holes where the spots had once been. Mum was looking like a big red balloon about to explode. Her eyes were like eggs sticking out of her head and her nose like a big red doorknob. Slowly she turned white with red spots, just like Lucy's dress, and then she suddenly sat down like a balloon that had just gone woosh and then gone saggy and crinkly.

'What's happening here?' said Dad as he put his head through the door. 'That's a pretty lace dress you have got on there my girl. Quick, get in the car. We're late. You all right Mum?' said Dad, noticing Lucy's mum sitting down catching her breath.

'Oh yes I'm fine, I think. Come on then. I'll just take another dress in case you want to change Lucy,' said Mum. Lucy had looked so proud of herself Mum thought it might be a good idea to forget about the holes, and to forget about feeling angry. They hopped into the car.

'Can you sew the red spots onto my bed when we get home tonight Mum?' said Lucy in the car. 'I promise that I won't take my bed to playcentre.'

Finny in Angerland

Warwick Pudney

Finny was shaking when he went to bed. He had been very angry today and he had felt like he had a ball of fire in his tummy. He was so angry that he felt scared.

He pulled the covers over his head and stared into the darkness of his bed. Blackness. He pushed the covers a little higher. It was good to be out of the other world and in his own bed-tent. He stared down the bed to see if he could see his toes. No toes, just a little red Humpalump dancing on his tummy.

What!

He stuck his head out from under the blankets into the cool bedroom air. He must be dreaming. He stuck his head back under to see if it was still there.

'Growly grumpy grumpadump, howly scowly humpalump,' stomped a little creature like a baby hippopotamus on his tummy.

'What are you doing here stomping on my tummy? Can you get off please? I have just had my dinner,' said Finny still amazed.

'Dinner, did you!' said the Humpalump. 'Dinner! Well you are just lucky! My owners haven't fed me for three days and my tummy is so growly and I am very, very upset and VERY angry.'

'Well I suppose you would be after three days,' said Finny. 'Can I help you?'

'Yes you can pick some wumpy off the wumpylumpy tree for me. You look very tall.' With that the Humpalump hopped off his tummy and headed off down the bottom of the bed. Finny turned in his bed and dived down after him. The darkness of his bed suddenly changed and he came out into a dark cave with bushes at the entrance and pale light coming through. He just caught a glimpse of a lumpy tail disappearing through it. Scrambling to his feet Finny grabbed the end of the tail and crashed through the entrance.

'Ouch you Tugalump. Let go of my tail. That makes me even more angry. If you had a tail I would bite it back.'

'Sorry. Sorry. I was afraid of getting lost. Where are we going?'

'Nowhere if you pull my tail you Finnylump,' said the Humpalump tucking his tail into his pocket for safety. 'Follow me,' and he lumped off up the path.

Finny lumped off after him only to suddenly hear a piercing shriek. 'Shraaaaaaaaak, Shraaaaaaaakitty-shraaaak.' He looked up above him and there in the branches of a tree was a tall, brightly feathered bird with a long, blue beak.

'Oh dear me, Shraaaaaaaketty-shraaaaak.' As the horrible crying filled his ears, Finny saw several big, blue tears roll down the bird's beak. They dripped off and landed splat on Finny's head.

'Stop, stop, before you go pop. Stop bird. You're drowning me,' said Finny. 'What's the matter?'

'The sneak-a-snake crawled up behind me and pulled out some of my tail feathers and I have a very sore bottom. It hurrrrts. Ohhhh, shraaaaaak, shraaaaaaak.'

'Stop, stop, before you go pop. Stop crying,' said Finny. 'I can't swim. Do you always cry when you get angry? Why don't you just get angry and use your big beak to screech loudly and tell the sneak-a-snake how sore your bottom is and if she does it again you will sit on her head.'

The shraaaketty bird suddenly stopped crying. 'Why didn't I think of that? I'll go and practise on that vine over there.'

Finny put his hands on his ears and ran to catch up with the Humpalump. He had just caught up when they passed a huge hill of boulders at the side of the track. There in the middle was Nostasaurus, a huge, purple beast the size of ten houses and a ship, leaping up and down on the boulders. Flames were coming out of his wild and angry eyes as he picked up rocks the size of cars and smashed them down so that they broke into little pieces. The earth shook with every step and wobbled like jelly when the Nostasaurus smashed the huge rocks like eggs.

'Stop, stop, before you go pop,' called Finny.

The Nostasaurus froze like a purple statue and looked around.

'Stop, stop, before you go pop,' called Finny.

The Nostasaurus looked puzzled then looked down and stared at Finny in the middle of his furious rock smashing.

'What are you so angry about Nostasaurus? There's an awful lot of shaking going on!'

The Nostasaurus looked dumbly down at Finny and he said in a very quiet, small voice, 'Er, aaah, my mother has forgotten to collect me from day care. And I don't like being on my own. I want my mummy.'

Finny patted his foot and said, 'There, there, baby Nostasaurus. I know what that is like. My mummy forgot me one day and I thought she had left me forever. But she hadn't. She just broke down in the car. She will remember you because she loves you. Just wait and see.'

The Nostasaurus sat down with a thump that shook the bananas off the trees and said, 'Do you really think so? Okay. I'll just sit here and wait for my mummy.' With that he put his giant arms about himself and gave himself a cuddle.

Finny and Humpalump rushed off up the track because the Humpalump was really hungry now and Finny didn't want him dancing on his tummy again. Just in time, around the corner, was the wumpylumpy tree. But there at the bottom were two hairy balls of arms and legs fighting, biting and tugamal-lighting so hard that Finny thought they might be one big angry fur ball.

Guess what he said…

'Stop, stop, before you go pop,' called Finny. Slowly the whizzing ball became still and two hairy faces stuck their noses out and said, 'What's up Finny?'

'What are you fighting for Utumutus?'

'He stole my eggnuts,' said one.

'He left them lying around,' said the other.

'Well I'll get you back for stealing you…'

'Stop, stop, before you go pop,' called Finny. 'You both made a mistake. Why don't you share?'

'Hmmmm,' said the black Utumutu.

'Hmmmm,' said the green Utumutu. 'Okay. Never thought of that!' and they gave each other such a hug, so hard, that Finny thought he would have to call, 'Stop, stop, before you go pop' again.

Quickly he picked the high branches of the wumpylumpy tree and passed the fruit to the hungry Humpalump.

'Yum, yum,' went Humpalump and stuck his nose right in one so the juice went over his face.

'Got to go now Humpalump. It must be about morning in my bed.'

'Thank you so much. It's much better having yummy in my tummy than snakes,' said Humpalump with his mouth full.

Finny dashed off along the path, into the cave, then squeezed up through the sheets of his bed. It felt and smelled so good lying there in the dark and he didn't feel angry any more. Better still, he didn't feel scared of other angry people any more. He didn't even feel scared of his own anger.

With a smile he snuggled down and dreamed of cuddling a big, soft, hairy, cuddly Nostasaurus called Ted.

Sara May gets dressed

Éliane Whitehouse

'Time to get up, Sara May,' said Mum.

'Now what will you wear today?'

'My bathing suit with the dots and spots.

That's what I'll wear today.'

'Your bathing suit is stretched and old and besides it's winter. You'll be too cold. Now what will you wear today?'

'I'll wear my pyjamas with frills and bows. I always feel warm when I'm wearing those. That's what I'll wear today.'

'Pyjamas are clothes that we wear to bed. You'll have to find something else instead. Now what will you wear today?'

'I shall wear my stretchy purple skirt and over the top Daddy's dark green shirt, and your belt with the bobbles, and my vest with the toggles. That's what I'll wear today.'

'Oh no!' said Mum. 'I'd be so embarrassed. Now go and get dressed. I'm feeling harassed. We're going shopping and to the library. Please wear something neat and tidy...and warm and clean.'

'Now please! No shocks! And don't forget your shoes and socks.'

'I'm ready now!' said Sara May.

'But I can't get my coat buttoned up today.'

'That's strange,' said Mum. 'It's much too tight. It fitted yesterday alright.'

'Oh Sara May,' said Mum. 'Oh dear! What are you wearing under there?'

'My bathing suit with dots and spots. My pyjamas with the frills and bows, my purple skirt and Daddy's shirt, your belt and my new vest with toggles.'

'I washed my face. My coat is warm. My shoes are on. And here I am! I'm dressed!'

The Berry Tree

Éliane Whitehouse

Mrs Malinki was very old. Her back was bent and her hair was wispy white. Everyone in the street knew Mrs Malinki and her garden. The children liked the trees that grew there.

In summer the children sat beneath the plum tree. The branches dripped their sweet, purple fruit. The children licked their sticky lips and walked home with red-smeared faces. Their parents said, 'I see you've been in Mrs Malinki's garden.'

In autumn the apples were shiny red and green globes and Mrs Malinki sat on her steps with her marmalade cat. She cut the codlin moth bugs from the children's fruit and they walked home with their mouths crammed full. Their parents said, 'We see you've been in Mrs Malinki's garden.'

In winter the tamarillo tree dropped its glossy red fruit on the grass. As the children stuffed their pockets and walked home Mrs Malinki called, 'Scoop out the fruit and sprinkle it with sugar.' When the children emptied their pockets in the kitchen their parents said, 'We see you've been in Mrs Malinki's garden.'

In spring when the daffodils starred the lawn the children picked and peeled the tart grapefruit to suck the segments.

But the best tree was outside Mrs Malinki's garden. It was the Berry Tree. Its berries were scarlet and hung in bunches like bead necklaces. The children knew not to eat the berries but the birds loved the tiny, red fruit. They thronged the tree and gorged themselves.

Most importantly the Berry Tree was a tree for climbing. Its branches were strong and wide and went up like a staircase to anywhere the children chose. On some days the tree was a pirate ship. On other days it was a castle. Often it was a place to just sit and look.

That was until the day Samantha broke her arm. That was the day Henry's father forgot to set his alarm clock and woke up late for work. He tripped over Henry's football on the way to the shower and roared at Henry as he pushed past him. So that was the day Henry yelled at his brother James who was buttering toast and James knocked over the marmalade. The marmalade splashed onto their mother's dress and she blamed Henry because she had to change her clothes before she went to work.

It was school holidays so Henry pushed his hands into his pockets and walked down the road to the Berry Tree. Melinda who was four and knew a lot, was sitting on the lowest branch talking to Mrs Malinki's marmalade cat whose name was Syrup. She said, 'Hello' to Henry, but he said, 'Huh' and climbed higher up the tree.

Samantha, who was six and made up stories, was further up the Berry Tree being the Princess Persimmon in her palace. Henry crashed through the branches.

'Mind my throne!' said Samantha.

'It's just a branch. It's not a stupid throne,' said Henry pushing past her.

'It is so too,' said Samantha.

'Is not,' said Henry and thumped her arm. Samantha grabbed at the tree trunk but it was too wide to hold on to and she slipped. She fell from one branch to another until she hit the ground.

Henry sat in the tree and shivered. He thought she was dead. Samantha lay on the ground and hurt all over. She thought she was dying. Melinda, who knew a lot, ran to Mrs Malinki who called an ambulance.

Samantha got a plaster cast on her arm and the children signed it, except for Melinda who drew a cat because she liked cats.

The next day lots of people gathered under the Berry Tree.

'This tree is dangerous,' said Samantha's mother. 'It has to go.'

'Oh no!' said Mrs Malinki in dismay. 'It's the children's playground and the birds eat the berries in the winter.'

'It's shady in the summer,' said James.

'Yeah! It's cool!' said Henry clicking his fingers.

Samantha was leaning against the trunk with her arm in plaster.

'Please don't cut it down,' she said. 'Mrs Malinki planted this tree on her wedding day and it's ever so old.'

'I've always thought this tree was too dangerous,' said Samantha's mother. She walked around the tree peering up through the branches. The man from the council scratched his head and looked thoughtful.

'We can't have people breaking limbs on council property,' he muttered. 'It will have to come down. I'll send someone out with a chain saw tomorrow.'

'But it's 60 years old,' said Mrs Malinki, her eyes filling with tears.

'Sorry lady,' said the man from the council. 'Safety first!'

'What a pity!' said the post lady passing by. 'It's a great place to shelter from a downpour.' And she rode on down the street on her bike.

The next day the tree feller arrived with a truck and a chainsaw. The people gathered around. The tree feller looked up at the tree.

'What a pity!' he said. 'It's a magnificent tree.'

'It's very dangerous,' responded Samantha's mother.

'Has to go,' said the man from the council.

The tree feller sighed and picked up his chainsaw. Mrs Malinki closed her eyes and held on tight to Syrup, her marmalade cat. But the cat did not like being squeezed so tightly. Suddenly he leapt from her arms straight into the tree. Mrs Malinki gasped.

'Heh!' called the tree feller. 'Somebody get that cat down. I can't cut down a tree with a cat in it.'

Then Henry had a good idea. He ran across to the tree, climbed up high and sat on a branch.

'I thought you went up to get the cat,' said the tree feller.

'No,' replied Henry. 'I came up here so that you can't cut down the tree.'

'Come down this instant!' said the man from the council. But Henry stayed up the tree.

Melinda, who was sitting on the curb said, 'You can't cut it down because Henry is up there.'

Then all the other children saw what Henry was doing and ran to the tree too. Soon the Berry Tree was full of children perched among the leaves like monkeys in the zoo. Not to be left out Samantha stood at the bottom leaning against the trunk.

The tree feller groaned. He went to the cab of his truck and rang on his cell phone.

'Help!' he said. 'I can't cut this tree down. It's full of kids and cats.'

The community constable arrived in his patrol car.

'Now then,' he said. 'What's going on here?'

They all spoke at once so the constable asked Samantha and she told him what had happened.

'A sad story!' said the constable. 'What a pity! And such a beautiful tree! Quite stupendous!'

'Sixty years old!' said Mrs Malinki sadly.

'But very dangerous!' said Samantha's mother.

Melinda, who was four and knew a lot, was hanging upside down from the lowest branch.

'The Berry Tree isn't dangerous,' she said. 'He is.' And she pointed at Henry.

'Only when I'm very angry,' replied Henry. 'It was Mum's fault! She yelled at me.'

'It was Henry's fault,' said his mother. 'He yelled at James.'

'It was Dad's fault,' said Henry. 'He pushed me.'

'It was Henry's fault,' said Henry's father. 'He left his ball in the hall. And besides, my alarm clock didn't go off.'

'You'd better cut down the alarm clock,' said the post lady passing by on her bike.

'She may be right,' said the man from the council. 'Perhaps the tree isn't dangerous after all.'

'No one's been hurt in 60 years,' said Mrs Malinki.

'But what if my daughter gets hurt again?' asked Samantha's mother.

'If everyone controls their temper she's safer up there than she is on the street,' replied the Constable.

'I suppose you're right,' sighed Samantha's mother.

'I told you so!' said Melinda who was right way up now.

Mrs Malinki smiled and went back into her garden to pick peaches. The marmalade cat climbed down the tree and followed her.

Barnaby's very bad word

Éliane Whitehouse

Barnaby did not like wearing his best clothes. His favourite clothes were his old shorts and his t-shirt with a sign on the front that read:

> This is my favourite shirt
>
> Do not wash it
>
> I want to wear it always.

But sometimes Mum and Dad made him wear his best clothes.

One day Dad said, 'Time to have a shower, Barnaby, and put on your best clothes. It's Great-Grandma's birthday party today.'

'I don't want to dress up,' said Barnaby.

'I know,' said Dad. 'But today is Great-Grandma's 90th birthday. Everyone will be wearing their best clothes.'

Lots of people were at Great-Grandma's party – Grandpa and Grandma, aunties and uncles and cousins by the dozen.

Mum had made a special, huge birthday cake with icing and a bow and 90 candles. Mum and Grandma lit the candles. Everyone sang 'Happy Birthday to You' and then Barnaby and two cousins helped Great-Grandma to blow out the candles.

'I don't have much puff these days,' said Great-Grandma.

Mum cut up the cake so that everyone could have a piece.

'Come along Barnaby,' said Mum. 'You can hand around the cake.'

Barnaby walked around very carefully with the big plate full of cake.

He knew that everyone was watching him. He didn't want to drop the plate.

Cousin Clare said, 'Can I have two pieces?'

Barnaby said, 'No!'

Cousin Clare reached out her hand to take another piece.

Barnaby turned around quickly to stop her and he collided with Aunty Jo. Down went the plate. Down went the cake onto the floor. And Barnaby yelled a bad word. It was a very bad word indeed. It was such a bad word that I can't write it here. Everyone gasped and spluttered. The cousins giggled.

And Mum and Dad shouted, 'Barnaby!' in very loud voices.

Barnaby was embarrassed. His face went bright red.

'Don't worry,' said Grandpa. 'I swear sometimes but I swear in the garden where no one can hear me.'

'What you need,' said Great-Grandma, 'is a swear word of your own that isn't bad.'

'Like fiddle dee dee!' said Aunty Floss.

'Or possum poo,' suggested Dad.

'Or sugar pops,' said Mum.

'No! No!' said Great-Grandma. 'Your own swear word needs to be something you don't like.'

'Broccoli,' said Barnaby. He stamped his foot to try out the word.

'Oh broccoli!' he said. 'No, it doesn't feel right.'

'Try something from school that you don't like,' Great-Grandma suggested.

'Spelling!' said Barnaby.

'Oh spelling!' he yelled stamping his foot. 'No, that's not right either.'

'Well now,' said Great-Grandma, 'what do you hate most of all?'

'Best clothes,' replied Barnaby.

'Well then,' said Great-Grandma, 'try that!'

'Best clothes!' yelled Barnaby stamping his foot. 'Yeah, best clothes!'

'Oh brussel sprouts!' shouted Cousin Clare.

'Oh dirty dishes!' shouted Grandma.

'Oh smelly socks!' yelled Mum.

Everyone joined in.

'Monday mornings', 'windy weather', 'rotten apples', 'ads on tele', 'catawauling cats'.

Grandpa sat down at the piano.

'Time for a swear dance!' he said pounding out a tune.

Everyone danced and stamped and shouted out their own swear word.

'Wet washing', 'soggy doggies', 'muddy foot prints'.

And 'Best clothes! Best clothes!' shouted Barnaby, the loudest of them all.

None of the characters in these stories are intended to resemble actual people and have been created to illustrate common dilemmas.

Grandpa's whiskers

Warwick Pudney

I hate kissing Grandpa
He has stickly whiskers
All over his face
I always get pricked
Can't find a clear place
But you make me kiss Grandpa
I feel angry when you...
Make me kiss Grandpa,
You know I don't want to
But there's one thing that's worse
In fact it's so bad
When you say to 'be nice'
I just feel so mad
That's kissing Grandma!
You say to 'behave'
But her whiskers are worse
'Cos she doesn't shave.

When I get angry...

Warwick Pudney

When I get angry...I get as angry as...
A snake with no dinner
A huge green pop-eyed monster
A hippopotamus who just stood on his own tail
A jumpy lumpy crab
A cat when the dog steals her meat
A grumpy rubbish-bin man
A bunny rabbit with one leg
A tiger who can't find his breakfast
A king eating mouldy old bread
A little girl who has lost her best shoes
And I want them right, right now!
RAAAAAHHHHHHHH!!!!!

Won't be angry then...

Éliane Whitehouse

When I'm angry I can…
stamp my feet
dance to the beat
beat on a drum
talk to my mum
thump my own bed
colour in red
paddle in a puddle
go to Dad for a cuddle.
Then when I am ready
I can sit and hug my teddy
and I won't be angry then.

Key Concepts

- Parents are fearful of anger because of negative past experiences and their own childhood. They don't need to be fearful. They should be calm and listen instead.

- Anger is an emotion. It's good, it's healthy and it's normal. We need it to protect and motivate ourselves. Parents and children can learn to live happily with it.

- Violence or abuse is behaviour. It is learned from others. It is not okay. It needs strong boundaries.

- Power, manipulation or control tactics that frighten, use or hurt people are abuse and are not okay.

- Behind anger there are feelings of hurt or fear or powerlessness.

- Bottled-up anger can become explosive, depressive and unpredictable in young children.

- We can learn the patterns, sensations, warnings and triggers of our anger before it is out of control.

- Close bonding and attachment allow a child to grow with safety and trust.

- Children act directly as a result of parenting. Parents need to get it right now, not later.

- Abuse can be physical, verbal, sexual, emotional or to property.

- There should be consequences for all abuse.

- Time out is for everyone's safety. Distraction, calming and nurture help children. A plan is still needed to fix the problem.

- We need to demonstrate the expression of our anger by safely using words and body movement.

- We need to help young children find out what is wrong and help them fix it.

- Parents and children need to learn that we don't always get what we want.

- Stress and fear increase our need to use anger for defence.

- Good self-esteem means we have less need for anger.

- Good listening helps dissipate anger and increase self-esteem.

- Children learn how to behave from adult models. They learn more from what adults *do* than what they say.

- Children have rights. It's not okay to use or abuse children.

- Talking about our feelings is healthy and reduces conflict.

- Other people's anger is their issue, and we can listen to them.

- Consistency is essential for parents keeping boundaries.

- Parents have extra power to use justly and responsibly.

- Labelling and putting down children is not okay.

- Anger rules keep everyone safe.

Some Questions You Might Ask

Some questions you might ask a counsellor, psychotherapist or yourself before you work with a child and parent:

- Do you work with parents of small children?
- Do you have regular supervision?
- Do you have children yourself?
- Are you father-friendly?
- Do you have training or experience with my culture?
- Are you a member of a professional organisation such as:
  - an association of psychotherapist
  - an association of counsellors
  - an association of child and adolescent psychotherapists
  - an association of social workers?
- What is your training for your work with parenting, children, babies? Diploma? Degree? Certificate?

About the Authors

Warwick Pudney

Warwick Pudney is the father of three grown children who, like him, have often felt angry and, like him, don't always get it right. He lives and works in New Zealand establishing relationship programmes, taking workshops, teaching at the Auckland University of Technology (AUT University), training and writing. He travels often to Europe to lecture and to see his Little Volcano grandchildren.

His favourite things to feel angry about are violence on television, children getting hurt, wars, books not being returned and someone else finishing the biscuits.

His main role is as a social change educator and therapist, working with men and boys in the field of anger, gender relations and fatherhood, and his passion is helping men live more creative lives. He also enjoys backpacking, travel, dancing, listening to music, canoeing, hiking, life and chocolate biscuits.

Éliane Whitehouse

Éliane Whitehouse regretfully passed away just months before the final publication of this book. She lived in Auckland, New Zealand. She had been a school teacher, a counsellor and a psychotherapist. Éliane worked with couples to improve family relationships and for many years facilitated parenting courses. She particularly liked the special times with her granddaughter. Éliane was a member of her city's Zero Tolerance to Violence group. She enjoyed writing and had two children's novels published: *Wood Smoke* and *Young Exile*.

Éliane: 'I guess what I feel angry about most is that in today's society parents often don't earn enough to look after their families and this means that they work long hours and don't have enough time to spend with their children.'

Since co-writing *Little Volcanoes* she suffered a debilitating illness. She was unable to take part in working on this edition of the book published by Jessica Kingsley Publishers in the UK.

References

Ainsworth, M.D.S. (1991) 'Attachments and Other Affectional Bonds across the Life Cycle.' In C.M. Parkes, J. Stevenson-Hinde and P. Marris (eds) *Attachment Across the Life Cycle*. New York: Routledge.

Ainsworth, M. and Salter, D. (2010) 'Security and Attachment.' In R. Volpe (ed.) *The Secure Child: Timeless Lessons in Parenting and Childhood Education*. Greenwich, CT: IAP Information Age Publishing.

Ainsworth, M.D.S., Bell, S.M. and Stayton, D.J. (1991) 'Infant–Mother Attachment and Social Development: "Socialisation" as a Product of Reciprocal Responsiveness to Signals.' In M. Woodhead, R. Carr and P. Light (eds) *Becoming a Person*. Florence, KY: Taylor & Frances/Routledge.

Ainsworth, M., Blehar, M., Waters, E. and Wall, S. (1978) *Patterns of Attachment: A Psychological Study of the Strange Situation*. Hillsdale, NJ: Lawrence Erlbaum Associates.

Bartley, M. (2006) *Capability and Resilience: Beating the Odds*. London: University College London, Department of Epidemiology and Public Health.

Beebe, B. and Lachmann, F.M. (2002) *Infant Research and Adult Treatment: Co-Constructing Interactions*. Hillsdale, NJ: The Analytic Press.

Belsky, J. (2002) 'Quantity counts: Amount of child care and children's socioemotional development.' *Developmental and Behavioral Pediatrics 23*, 3, 167–170.

Biddulph, S. (1995) *Manhood: An Action Plan for Changing Men's Lives*. Sydney: Finch.

Biddulph, S. (2002) *Manhood: An Action Plan for Changing Men's Lives* (third edition). Lane Cove, NSW: Finch Publishing.

Biddulph, S. (2003) *Raising Boys*. London: Harper Thorsons.

Biddulph, S. (2008) *Raising Boys: Why Boys Are Different – and How to Help Them Become Happy and Well-Balanced Men*. Berkeley, CA: Ten Speed Press.

Blankenhorn, D. (1995) *Fatherless America: Confronting Our Most Urgent Social Problem*. New York: Harper Perennial.

Bowlby, J. (1973) *Separation: Anxiety and Anger*. New York: Basic Books.

Brandell, J.R. and Ringel, S. (2007) *Attachment and Dynamic Practice: An Integrative Guide for Social Workers and Other Clinicians*. New York: Columbia University Press.

Bridgman, G. (1998) *Analysis of the Australian Data from the Cartoon Network's New GenerAsians Survey*. Presented to the Sydney release of data from the 12 Asian nation study of youth attitudes, perceptions and behaviours, Sydney.

Briere, J. (2003) *Posttraumatic Stress Disorder*. Vancouver: International Medical News Group.

Chapman, P., McIntosh, C. and Mitchell, D. (2000) *Real Dads, Real Men: A Study of Fathers' Experiences of Child and Family Services in the Nelson/Tasman Region and their Suggestions for 'Father Friendly Services'*. Nelson: Nelson Marlborough Health Services.

Clarke-Stewart, K.A. (1978) 'And daddy makes three: The father's impact on mother and young child.' *Child Development 49*, 466–478.

Cline, F. (1979) *Understanding and Treating the Severely Disturbed Child*. Evergreen, CO: EC Publications.

Coen, M. (2011) 'Attachment disorder: Symptoms.' Available at www.attachmentandtrauma specialists.com/attachment_disorder/symptoms, accessed on 18 August 2011.

Diemer, G.A. (1997) 'Expectant fathers: Influence of perinatal education on stress, coping and spousal relations.' *Research in Nursing and Health 20*, 4, 281–293.

Eriksen, E.H. (1963) *Childhood and Society.* London: Hogarth Press.

Fancourt, R. (2000) *Brainy Babies.* Auckland: Penguin.

Fatherhood Institute (2010) *Fathers' Impact on Their Children's Learning and Achievement. Abergavenny: Fatherhood Institute.* Available at www.fatherhoodinstitute.org/2010/fatherhood-institute-research-summary-fathers-and-their-childrens-education, accessed on 30 September 2011.

Feeney, J.A. (1999) 'Adult attachment, emotional control, and marital satisfaction.' *Personal Relationships 6*, 169–185.

Fergusson, D. and Lynsky, M.T. (1997) 'Physical punishment/maltreatment during childhood and adjustment in young adulthood.' *Childhood Abuse and Neglect 21*, 7, 617–630.

Fonagy, P. (2001) *Attachment Theory and Psychoanalysis.* New York: Other Press.

Frodl, T., Reinhold, E., Koutsouleris, N., Donohoe, G. *et al.* (2010) 'Childhood stress, serotonin transporter gene and brain structures in major depression.' *Neuropsychopharmacology 35*, 6, 1383–1390.

Gilligan, J. (2001) *Preventing Violence: Prospects for Tomorrow.* London: Thames and Hudson Ltd.

Goldman, R. (2005) *Fathers' Involvement in their Children's Education.* London: National Family and Parenting Institute.

Grossmann, K., Grossmann, K.E., Fremmer-Bombik, E., Kindler, H., Scheuerer- Englisch, H. and Zimmermann P. (2002) 'The uniqueness of the child-father attachment relationship: Fathers' sensitive and challenging play as a pivotal variable in a 16-year longitudinal study.' *Social Development 11*, 3, 307–331.

Gurian, M. (2002) *Boys and Girls Learn Differently.* New York: Putnam.

Gurian, M. and Stevens, K. (2005) *The Minds of Boys: Saving Our Sons From Falling Behind in School and Life.* San Francisco, CA: Jossey-Bass.

Halle, C., Dowd, T., Fowler, C., Rissel, K. *et al.* (2008) 'Supporting fathers in the transition to parenthood.' *Contemporary Nurse 31*, 1, 57–70.

Hanh, T.N. (1987) *The Miracle of Mindfulness.* Boston, MA: Beacon Press.

Hanson, S., Hunter, L.P., Borman, J.R. and Sobo, E.J. (2009) 'Paternal fears of childbirth: A literature review.' *Journal of Perinatal Education 18*, 4, 12–20.

Hendrix, H. (1988) *Getting the Love You Want: A Guide for Couples.* New York: Henry Holt & Co.

Hendrix, H. (1990) *A Guide for Couples.* New York: Perennial.

Hoskins, L.L., Roth, R.M. and Giancola, P.R. (2010) 'Neuroimaging of Aggression: Empirical Findings and Implications.' In A. MacNeill Horton and L.C. Hartlage (eds) *Handbook of Forensic Neuropsychology* (second edition). New York: Springer Publishing Co.

Ilardi, S. (2009) *The Depression Cure.* Cambridge, MA: Da Capo Press.

Irwin, L., Siddiqi, A. and Hertzman, C. (2007) *Early Childhood Development: A Powerful Equaliser.* Vancouver: Commission for the Social Determinants of Health, World Health Organization.

James, A. (2007) *Teaching the Male Brain: How Boys Think, Feel, and Learn in School.* Thousand Oaks, CA: Corwin Press.

Jurkovic, G.J. (1997) *Lost Childhoods: The Plight of the Parentified Child.* London: Psychology Press.

Karen, R. (1990a) *Becoming Attached, Unfolding the Mystery of the Infant–Mother Bond and its Impact on Later Life.* New York: Warner Books.

Karen, R. (1990b) 'Becoming attached.' *The Atlantic Monthly*, February, 35–70.

Karen, R. (1998) *Becoming Attached: First Relationships and How They Shape Our Capacity to Love.* Oxford: Oxford University Press.

Karr-Morse, R. and Wiley, M.S. (1997) *Ghosts from the Nursery: Tracing the Roots of Violence.* New York: Atlantic Monthly Press.

Kitzinger, S. (2005) *Understanding Your Crying Baby.* London: Carroll & Brown.

Lamb, M.E. (1976) 'Interactions between two-year-olds and their mothers and fathers.' *Psychological Reports 38*, 447–450.

Lamb, M.E. (1977) 'Father-infant and mother-infant interaction in the first year of life.' *Child Development 48*, 167–181.

Lawson, D.M. (2008) 'Attachment, interpersonal problems, and family of origin functioning: Differences between partner violent and nonpartner violent men.' *Psychology of Men and Masculinity 9*, 2, 90–105.

McElligott, M. (2001) 'Fathercraft: Antenatal information wanted by first-time fathers.' *British Journal of Midwifery 9*, 9, 556–558.

Main, M. and Weston, D.M. (1981) 'The quality of the toddler's relationship to mother and to father: Related to conflict behavior and the readiness to establish new relationships.' *Child Development 52*, 932–940.

Main, M., Kaplan, N. and Cassidy, J. (1985) 'Security in infancy, childhood and adulthood: A move to the level of representation.' *Monographs of the Society for Research in Child Development 50*, 66–104.

Makinen, J.A. and Johnson, S.M. (2006) 'Resolving attachment injuries in couples using emotionally focused therapy: Steps toward forgiveness and reconciliation.' *Journal of Consulting and Clinical Psychology 74*, 6, 1114–1121.

Maldonado-Durán, J.M. (2002) *Infant and Toddler Mental Health: Models of Clinical Intervention with Infants and Their Families.* Washington, DC: American Psychiatric Publishing, Inc.

Meyers, S.A. and Landsberger, S.A. (2002) 'Direct and indirect pathways between adult attachment style and marital satisfaction.' *Personal Relationships 9*, 159–172.

Miller, L. (1997) *Understanding Your 4 Year-Old.* Redwood City, CA: Warwick Publishing.

Mitchell, D. and Chapman, P. (2002) *Dads: Part of the Team or Warming the Bench?* Nelson: Marlborough District Health Board.

Nathanson, D. (1992) *Shame and Pride: Affect, Sex and the Birth of Self.* New York and London: W.W. Norton.

NICHD ECCRN (Early Child Care Research Network) (2001) 'Further explorations of the detected effects of quantity of early child care on socioemotional adjustment.' Biennial Meeting of the Society for Research in Child Development. Minneapolis, MN: NICHD ECCRN.

Pace, U. and Zappulla, C. (2010) 'The role of insecure attachment, depression, behavioral problems and suicidal ideation in adolescence.' *Psicologia Clinica dello Sviluppo 14*, 3, 553–576.

Perry, B.D. (1997) 'Incubated in Terror: Neurodevelopment Factors in the Cycle of Violence.' In J. Osofsky (ed.) *Children in a Violent Society.* New York: Guilford Press.

Perry, B.D. (2008) 'Child Maltreatment: A Neurodevelopmental Perspective on the Role of Trauma and Neglect in Psychpathology.' In T.P. Beauchaine and S.P. Hinshaw (eds) *Child and Adolescent Psychopathology.* Hoboken, NJ: John Wiley & Sons.

Perry, B.D. (2009) 'Examining child maltreatment through a neurodevelopmental lens: Clinical applications of the Neurosequential Model of Therapeutics.' *Journal of Loss and Trauma 14*, 4, 240–255.

Plantin, L., Olukoya, A.A. and Ny, P. (2011). 'Positive health outcomes of fathers' involvment in pregnancy and childbirth paternal support: A scope study literature review.' *Fathering 9*, 1, 87–102.

Pruett, K. (2002) *Father-need.* New York: Broadway Books.

Pruett, K. and Pruett, M.K. (2009) *Partnership Parenting: How Men and Women Parent Differently – Why it Helps Your Kids and Can Strengthen Your Marriage.* Cambridge, MA: Da Capo Press.

Pudney, W. (2002) *Anger and Anti-Social Behaviour in New Zealand Schools.* Auckland: New Zealand Peace Foundation.

Pudney, W. (2005) *The Volcano Manual: A Profesional Helper's Guide for Using a Volcano in my Tummy.* Auckland: The Peace Foundation.

Pudney, W. and Whitehouse, É. (2000) *Adolescent Volcanoes: Helping Adults and Adolescents to Handle Anger.* Auckland: The Peace Foundation.

Pudney, W. and Whitehouse, É. (2003) *A Volcano in my Tummy: A Teachers', and Parents' Guide to Working with Children's Anger.* Auckland: The Peace Foundation.

Rush, E. and La Nauze, A. (2006) *The Sexualisation of Children in Australia.* Discussion Paper no. 90. Bruce. The Australia Institute.

Sax, L. (2006) *Why Gender Matters: What Parents and Teachers Need to Know about the Emerging Science of Sex Difference.* New York: Broadway Books.

Schore, A.N. (1994) *Affect Regulation and the Origin of the Self: The Neurobiology of Emotional Development.* Hillsdale, NJ: Lawrence Erlbaum Associates.

Sedlak, A.J. and Broadhurst, D. (1996) *Executive Summary of the Third National Incidence Study of Child Abuse and Neglect.* Maryland: U.S. Department of Health and Human Services, National Center on Child Abuse and Neglect.

Sidorowicz, L.S. and Lunney, G. (1980) 'Baby X revisited.' *Sex Roles 6,* 1, 67–73.

Steele, H., Steele, M., Croft, C. and Fonagy, P. (1999) 'Infant–mother attachment at one year predicts children's understanding of mixed emotions at six years.' *Social Development 8,* 161–178.

Whitehouse, É. and Pudney, W. (1996) *A Volcano in my Tummy: Helping Children to Handle Anger.* Gabriola Island: New Society Publishers.

Whitehouse, É. and Pudney, W. (2003) *Little Volcanoes.* Auckland: Peace Foundation.

Wilkinson, R.G. and Pickett, K. (2009) *The Spirit Level: Why More Equal Societies Almost Always Do Better.* London: Allen Lane

Winnicott, D.W. (1964) *The Child, the Family and the Outside World.* Reading, MA: Addison-Wesley.

Winnicott, D.W. (1971) *Therapeutic Consultations in Child Psychiatry.* London: The Hogarth Press and the Institute of Psycho-Analysis.

Winnicott, D.W. (1980) 'The Piggle: An Account of the Psychoanalytic Treatment of a Little Girl.' In I. Ramzy (ed.) *The International Psycho-Analytical Library 107,* 1–201. London: The Hogarth Press and the Institute of Psycho-Analysis.

World Health Organization (2002) *World Report on Violence and Health.* Geneva: WHO.

Further Reading

Duffield, N. (1999) *Talking to Kids About Divorce: A Book for Adults and Children*. London: Random House.

Erikson, E.H. (1980) *Identity and the Life Cycle*. New York: W.W. Norton & Company.

Families Commission, The (2009) *Family Violence Statistics Report*. Wellington: The Families Commission.

Fancourt, R. (2000) *Brainy Babies*. Auckland: Penguin.

Gianforte-Mansfield, L. and Waldmann, C.H. (1994) *Don't Touch my Heart: Healing the Pain of an Unattached Child*. Colorado Springs, CO: Pinon Press.

Gilligan, J. (2001) *Preventing Violence: Prospects for Tomorrow*. London: Thames and Hudson.

Green, C. (1985) *Toddler Taming: A Survival Guide for Parents*. New York: Fawcett Columbine.

Gurian, M. (2002) *Boys and Girls Learn Differently*. New York: Putnam.

Miller, L. (1997) *Understanding Your Four Year Old*. Redwood City, CA: Warwick Publishing.

Perry, B.D. (2002) *Violence and Childhood: How Persisting Fear Can Alter the Developing Child's Brain*. In D. Schetky and E. Benedek (eds) *Principles and Practice of Child and Adolescent Forensic Psychiatry*. Washington, DC: American Psychiatric Press Inc.

Reid, S. (1997) *Understanding Your Two Year Old*. Redwood City, CA: Warwick Publishing.

Schore, A. (2001) 'Effects of a secure attachment relationship on right brain development, affect regulation, and infant mental health.' *Journal of Infant Mental Health 22*, 201–269.

Stassen Berger, K. (1998) *The Developing Person Through the Life Span*. New York: Worth Publishers.

Viorst, J. (1971) *The Tenth Good Thing About Barney*. London: Collins.

Whitehouse, É. and Pudney, W. (1994, 1999, 2002) *A Volcano in My Tummy*. Auckland: The Peace Foundation.

Subject Index

abuse 139–40, 174–6
anger
  causes of 125–34, 137–40
  coping with 103–5
  deep anger 79
  and empathy 38–46
  and fathers 188–9, 191–2
  and gender 32–3
  grief 125–8
  immediate anger 77–8
  key concepts 210–11
  left by parent 132–4
  levels of 75–7
  parental responses to 11–12
  parental separation 129–32
  poems about 208–9
  right to feel 121–2
  stacked anger 78–9
  stories about 193–207
  vocabulary 47, 72–4
  warning signs for 89–93
anger responses
  drawing pictures 107–10
  exercise 106–7
Anger Rules 146–7
Anger Scale 75–7, 79–80
anger tracking
  expression of anger 86–7
  flow diagram for 83–4
  and powerlessness 85–6, 87
  success of 87–9
assumptions
  and empathy 43–4
attachment
  and childcare centres 138–9,
    142–4
  critics of theory 143–4
  importance of 13–14
  infancy 18–19
  pre-birth 17
  pre-school 23–6
  problems with 16–17
  toddlers 19–23

attachment disorders
  symptoms of 15–16

boredom
  avoiding 69–72
boundaries
  and child's changing needs
    57
  and communication 55
  and consequences 55–6
  consistency in 56
  description of 52–3
  and gender 57–8
  setting proper 53–5
boys
  and boundary setting 57–8
  challenging stereotypes 33–4
  co-operation with 62
  emotional life of 30–2
  and fathers 186, 189–91
  and fighting 111
  and parental separation 131
  and 'protector' role 32–3

calming nurture 98–9
calming techniques
  adult calmness 97–8
  calming nurture 98–9
  distraction 95
  expressiveness 95–7
  forms of 94
  parental calmness 97–8
childcare centres
  Anger Rules 146–7
  approaches to destructive
    behaviour 141–2
  and attachment 138–9,
    142–4
  first visit to centres 135–7
  reasons for anger in centres
    137–40
  working with parents 144–6

child abuse 139–40
  definitions of 174–6
children
  avoiding boredom 69–72
  and boundary setting 52–8
  checklist for raising happy
    168–9
  coping with anger 103–5
  establishing co-operation
    with 58–62
  and extended families
    176–83
  fighting between 110–13
  gender differences in 30–4
  importance of attachment
    13–14
  infancy attachment 18–19
  parental influence on 65–7
  and play 27–30
  pre-birth attachment 17
  pre-school attachment 23–6
  problems with attachment
    16–17
  relationship with parent 48
  resilience building 67–8
  right to feel anger 121–2
  toddler attachment 19–23
  treated as adult 163–4
  unconditional love for 68
  and violence 34–8, 140
communication
  and anger vocabulary 47
  and boundaries 55
  four-part phrase 49–52
  importance of 46
  listening skills 47–8
co-operation
  establishment of 58–62
consequences
  and boundary setting 55–6
  for mistakes 62–5

Author Index